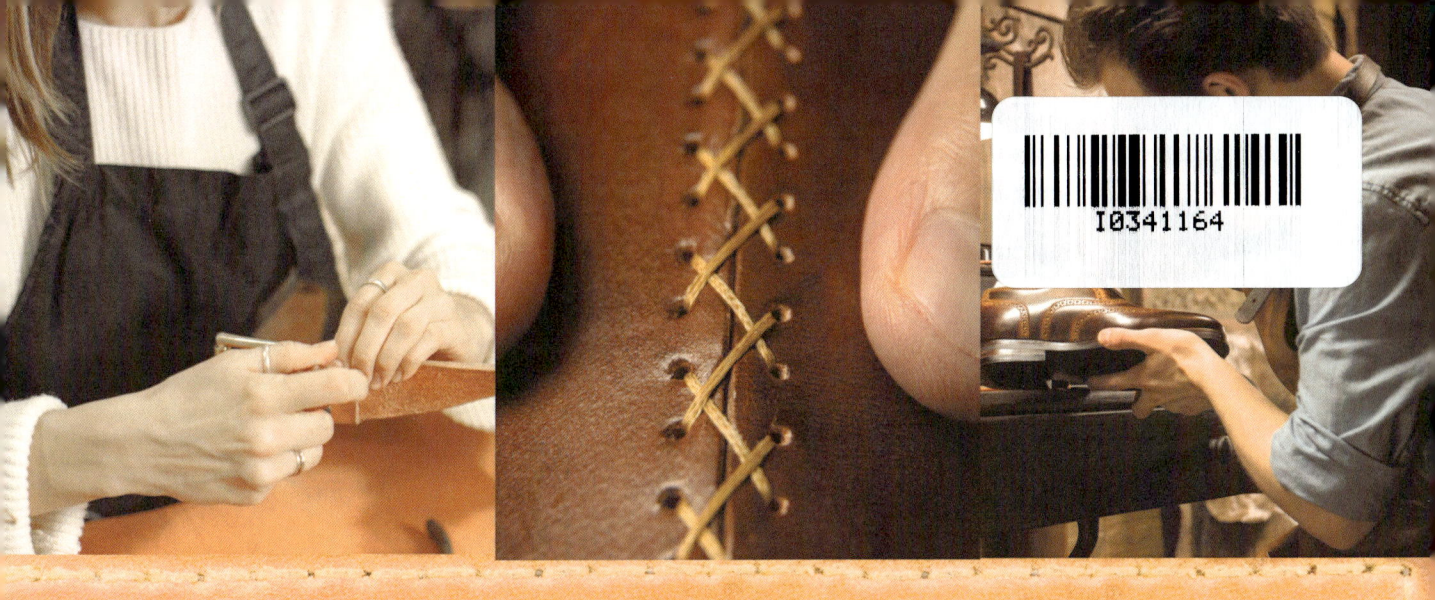

Leather Crafting Book-101

STEP-BY-STEP LEATHER CRAFT PROCESS, TOOLS, TIPS, AND LEATHER WORKING PROJECTS FOR BEGINNERS, YOUNG ADULTS, AND TEENS

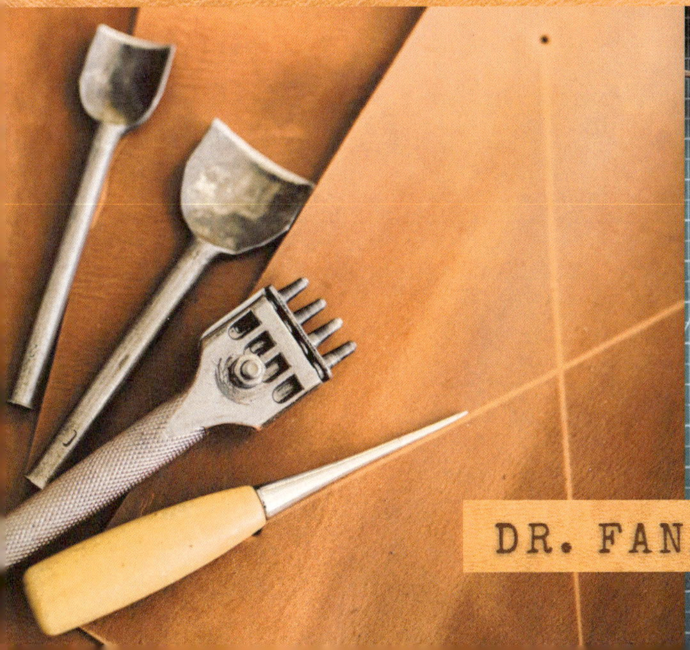

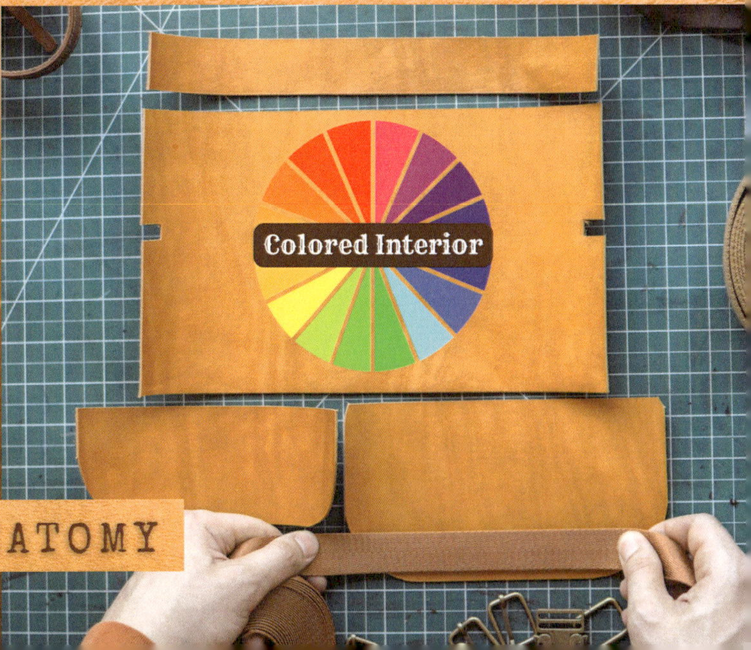

Colored Interior

DR. FANATOMY

copyright@ dr. fanatomy 2023

All rights reserved. No part of this publication may be reproduced, distributed, or transmitted in any form or by any means, including photocopying, recording, or other electronic or mechanical methods, without the prior written permission of the publisher, except in the case of brief quotations embodied in critical reviews and certain other noncommercial uses permitted by copyright law.

This book is a work of non-fiction , and any resemblance to actual persons, living or dead, or actual events is purely coincidental.

The information and techniques described in this book are intended for educational and informational purposes only. The author and publisher shall not be held liable for any injury, damage, or loss arising from the use or misuse of the information presented in this book.

While every effort has been made to ensure the accuracy of the information contained within this book, the author and publisher make no warranties or representations, express or implied, about the completeness, accuracy, reliability, suitability, or availability with respect to the contents of this book for any purpose. The use of any information provided in this book is at the reader's own risk.

BONUS BOOKLET - LEATHERWORKING

Thanks for purchasing the book, and welcome to the community! We are providing Bonus Booklet which contains :

- 10 Beginner Frequently Questions (FAQs) with answers.
- Top 10 Recommended Youtube Channels
- Patterns and Designs for a few initial projects

Click Here/copy this link: https://bit.ly/FanatomyLWBonus

Else you can scan the below bar code

TABLE OF CONTENTS

1. THE WHY-INTRODUCTION TO THE WORLD OF LEATHER CRAFTING

   - WHAT IS LEATHERWORKING
   - HISTOY- 10 INTERESTING FACTS
   - SOURCES OF LEATHER
   - GRADES OF LEATHER
   - LEATHERWORKING IN CURRENT TIMES-WHY?
   - TOP 3 BEGINNER MISTAKES

2. THE DEVICES-WORKSPACE, TOOLS & MATERIALS

   - SETTING UP AN IDEAL WORKSPACE
   - TYPES OF TOOLS
   - CUTTING TOOLS
   - PUNCHING TOOLS
   - SEWING TOOLS
   - EDGING TOOLS
   - DYING AND FINISHING TOOLS
   - OTHER MISC. TOOLS

3. THE HOW- LEATHERWORKING PROCESSES/STEPS

   - LEATHERWORKING PROCESS TABLE
   - MAKING SIMPLE CARD HOLDER -UNDERSTANDING PROCESSES

TABLE OF CONTENTS

4. GETTING STARTED - PROCESSES IN DETAILS

- DRAWING PATTERNS/DESIGNS & CUTTING
- PUNCHING HOLES
- DESIGN TRANSFER
- DECORATING LEATHER(TOOLING)
- STITCHING
- FINISHING

5. LEATHERWORKING SAFETY- BASIC GUIDELINES

- SAFETY AND FIRST AID IN LEATHERWORKING
- TIPS FOR SAFETY
- CUTS AND SCRATCHES
- INFLAMMATION
- POISONING
- BEST PRACTICES

6. LET'S MAKE SOMETHING - 10 STARTER PROJECTS

- SIMPLE KEYCHAIN
- BRACELET FROM AN OLD BELT
- COIN POUCH
- PEN COVER
- PASSPORT COVER
- CUTE HEART RING
- CLASSY COASTER
- DESK PAD
- SUNGLASS CASE
- CARD HOLDER

TABLE OF CONTENTS

7. TIPS & FAQS

- 20 TIPS FOR BEGINNER LEATHER CRAFTER
- BEGINNER FREQUENTLY ASKED QUESTIONS (FAQS)

8. APPENDIX

- APPENDIX 1: LEATHER SUPPLIERS LIST
- APPENDIX 2: INCHES TO MM CONVERSION TABLE
- APPENDIX 3: ONLINE RESOURCES
- APPENDIX 4: GLOSSARY

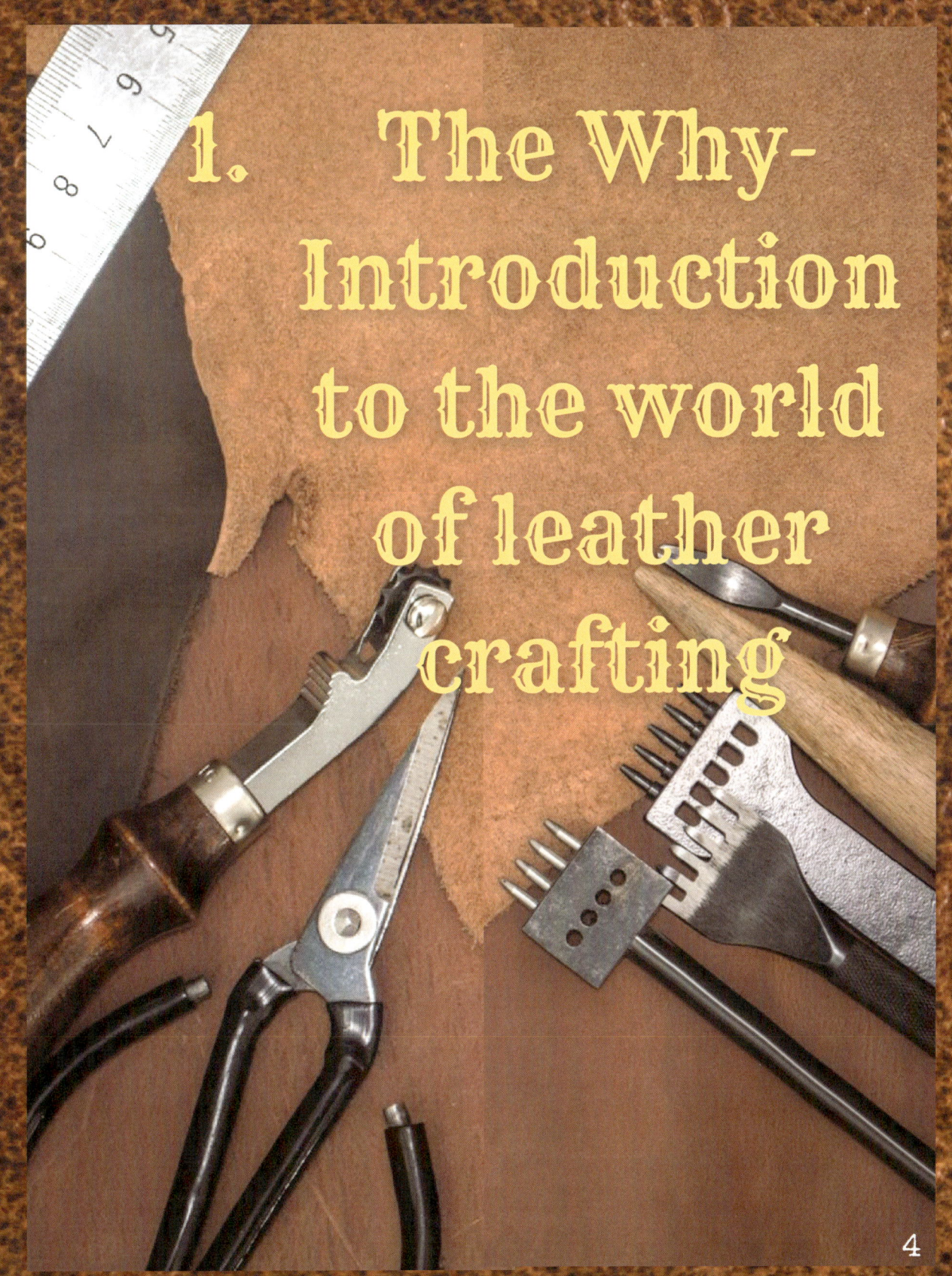

1. The Why- Introduction to the world of leather crafting

From the beginning of human civilization to today's high-tech world, natural leather has offered and enriched the lives of humans in many ways.

No other natural material offers so many options, whether you are interested in making designs in natural leather or making articles to be made use of or put on: like belts, shoes, pocketbooks, sporting devices, horse equipment, garments, shield, sheaths, holsters, drums, and also bags; leather is one of the most functional and resilient products.

It can be built, formed, embellished, laced, sewed, glued, attached, colored, and completed in various ways.

So you are encouraged to use your creativity and have a good time!

What is Leather working?

Leatherworking is the art and craft of producing items from leather. It entails collaborating with different types of leather to create useful or attractive things such as wallets, bags, belts, shoes, and more.

Leatherworking has been around for centuries and has a rich history across societies and continents.

Leatherworking is an essential craft due to its flexibility and sturdiness. Leather is a product that can last for years if properly taken care of, making it a valuable option for lots of day-to-day products. Beyond its performance, leatherworking likewise provides a possibility for creative expression. With suitable devices and techniques, leatherworkers can produce unique, attractive items that display their style and vision.

If you're new to leatherworking, do not be intimidated!

You can become efficient in this satisfying craft with some practice and perseverance.

Throughout this book, we'll provide you with the understanding and abilities necessary to begin developing your natural leather projects.

We'll cover the products and tools required and the methods used and provide beginner-friendly jobs to aid you in getting going. So let's dive in and also start exploring the world of leatherworking!

History of Leatherworking - 10 interesting facts

- Leatherworking goes back to prehistoric times, with proof of leather footwear in historical sites dating back over 8,000 years.

- The old Egyptians were understood for their leatherworking abilities and produced a wide range of leather goods, including shoes, apparel, and bags.

- In old Greece, leather was frequently used for armor and as a covering for shields.

- During the Middle Ages, leatherworking became a vital profession, with tanners and leatherworkers creating leather items for various uses, consisting of apparel and armor for knights and soldiers.

- Leatherworking guilds were developed in Europe throughout the Center Ages to manage the profession and guarantee top-quality requirements were fulfilled.

- Leatherworking played an essential duty in the American Transformation, with natural leather items such as footwear and cartridge boxes.

- The Industrial Change caused the mechanization of natural leather manufacturing, enabling mass production of natural leather products and making the leather much more economical and available.

- Leatherworking has been used in various forms of art and layout, including in the creation of leather-bound books and in the apparel industry.

- The process of tanning leather has developed with time, with very early techniques utilizing all-natural products such as tree bark, while modern-day methods use synthetic chemicals.

- Today, leatherworking stays a prominent craft, with individuals throughout the globe utilizing leather to produce practical and decorative products such as bags, shoes, and furniture.

Tanning circa 1880
(By Anonymous artist – http://www.digibib.tu-bs.de/?docid=00000286, Public Domain, https://commons.wikimedia.org/w/index.php?curid=981570)

Sources of Leather

Based on the animals from which leather comes, we can split it into 2 categories:

Leather from Domestic Animal	Leather from Wild Game Animals
Domestic animals like Cows, pigs, and sheep are the main source of leather 	Wild animals such as deer, elk, moose, bison, and kangaroo additionally give skins for leatherworking usage. Some are raised commercially, but most are taken in the wild by hunters who comply with federal and state regulations to ensure the animals' continued survival.

Tanning is the process of turning hides right into durable and long-lasting genuine leather.

It includes cleansing, saturating, and treating the hides with a tanning agent (either all-natural or chemical) to make the natural leather solid and resistant to deterioration.

 The leather is after that dried, extended, and completed to give it the desired density, softness, and shade.

This process is essential in natural leather craft because it changes raw animal hides right into a beneficial product that can be used to produce a range of items like shoes, belts, bags, and furniture.

Tanned leather in Marrakesh
(By DonarReiskoffer, CC BY-SA 3.0, https://commons.wikimedia.org/w/index.php?curid=458235)

Types of Leather

(1) Vegetable-tanned leather

This leather is tanned with the help of extracts from tree bark and is used for things that require rigid, natural solid leather. It is the only natural leather that can be tooled. Veg-tanned natural leather is mainly used in hand leathercrafting like natural leather sculpting, shield, saddlery, shoemaking, and bookbinding.

(2) Chrome-tanned leather

Chrome-tanned leather has been tanned with chemicals containing chromium salts and is usually used for products that ask for soft, exceptionally adaptable natural leather. It is different from veg-tanned leather primarily because it can not be tooled.

Chrome-tanned natural leather creates most of the leather products you see, specifically garments, purses, and furniture.

Veg-Tanned	Chrome-Tanned
<ul><li>Natural materials like tree bark to tan the leather slowly and carefully.</li><li>Color-natural tan</li><li>More durable and long-lasting & can withstand more wear and tear.</li><li>Eco-friendly process</li><li>More expensive</li></ul>	<ul><li>Uses chemicals like chromium salts to tan</li><li>Color-bluish tint</li><li>Less durable than veg-tanned</li><li>Toxic to environment</li><li>Less Expensive</li></ul>

Rawhide: The animal hide that has been de-haired and treated but not tanned is called Rawhide. It is a stiff product that needs to be placed in water to become usable.

It becomes hard as well as holds its shape once it dries. It is used to make drumheads, water containers, moccasin soles, and also parts of saddles.

One beginner issue while purchasing leather: Most natural leather distributors won't cut and offer smaller pieces. It can make purchasing natural leather expensive and limit the variety of weights and colors you can use in one job.

Solution:

- You can find a leather vendor that will give you project-based leather pieces.
- Befriend a fellow beginner and share the big leather piece.
- Look for leather scraps, and they are useful in doing a few initial projects and practicing.
- Use restored leather. Second-hand store purses, layers, belts, and various other accessories can be a wonderful source of chrome-tanned natural leather scraps.

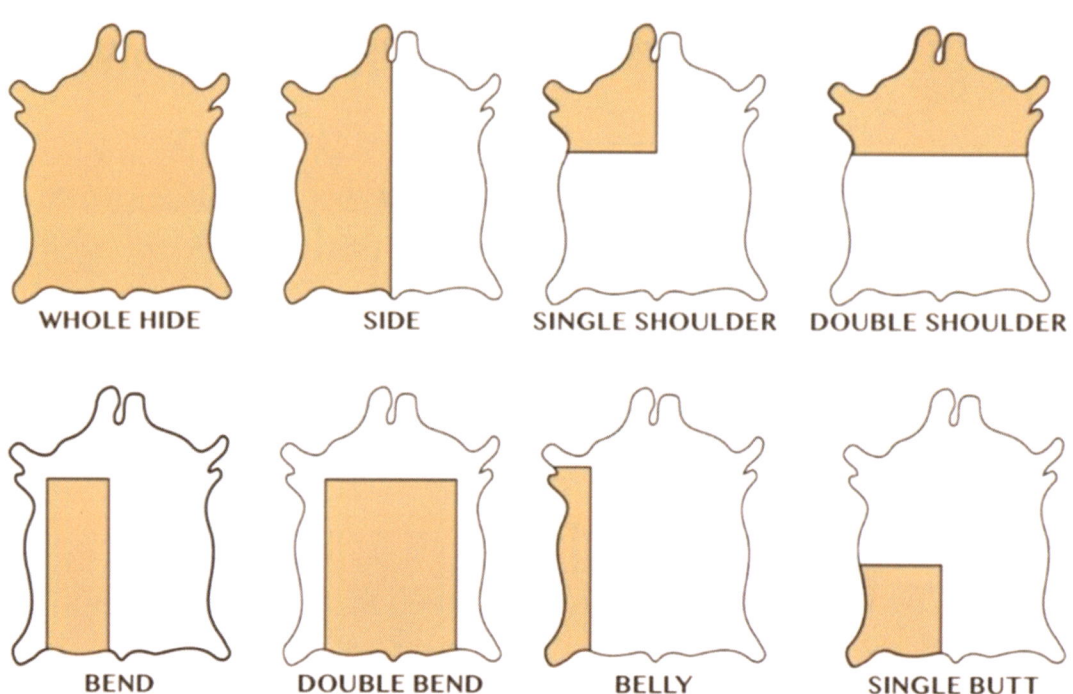

Parts of Hide

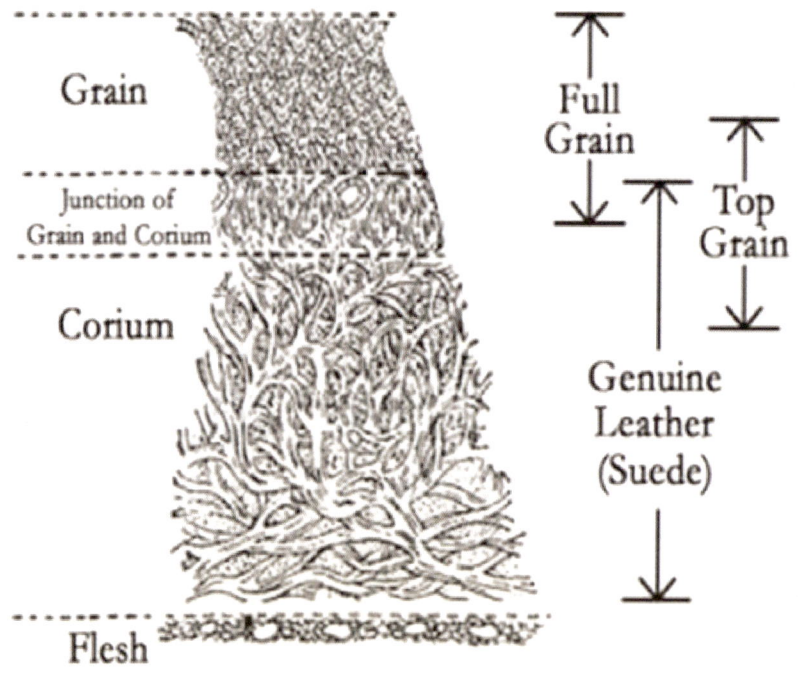

Sections of Hide

Grades of Leather

The grades of leather are based on the quality and features of the animal hide utilized to make the natural leather. The animal hide comes from cows, pigs, goats, lamb, and various other animals, and it goes through a series of processes to change it into leather.

Full-grain leather: It is the best quality of leather from the top layer of the hide, which is the strongest and most sturdy component. It is the most natural-looking and also develops a patina over time. Used for making- belts, budgets, bags, shoes, and leather coats.

Top-grain leather: Top-grain leather is the second-highest high-quality leather made from the external layer of the animal hide, which is sanded and buffed to get rid of flaws.

It is smooth and uniform in look, and also it is less sturdy than full-grain leather. Used for making- brief-cases, travel luggage, furniture, and leather coats.

Genuine leather: It is made from the lower layers of the hide and is cheaper than full-grain or top-grain leather. It is usually coated with a layer of polyurethane to improve its look and toughness. Used for making - watch bands, bags, and little leather accessories.

Bonded leather: It is made from scraps of leather ground up and bonded with polyurethane. It is the most affordable quality of leather and could be more durable. Used for making inexpensive things such as book covers, desk devices, and affordable furnishings.

The major differences between these grades of leather are their longevity, look, and price.

Full-grain leather is one of the most sturdy and natural-looking, yet it is likewise the most costly. Genuine and top-grain leather is less long-lasting and costly than full-grain leather, yet they are still high-quality options. Bonded leather is the least costly and also the least long-lasting alternative. You can use the below. sample label to collect types of leather and paste it in your first notebook of leatherworking .

Leather Sample

_____
Type of leather

_____
Tannage (vegetable, chrome, etc.)

_____
Thickness characteristics

Uses: _____

_____

_____

_____

Why Leatherworking in current times?

Innovative Outlet: Leatherworking lets you reveal your creativity and create distinct, customized things. This can be an excellent method to unwind and de-stress after a lengthy day.

Sustainability: With the rising awareness of sustainability and the influence of quick fashion on the atmosphere, leatherworking enables you to develop durable and long-lasting things.

Cost-efficient: Leatherworking can additionally be a cost-effective way to acquire high-grade natural leather products. By making your leather products, you can save money and produce products that fulfill your details needs and choices.

Skill Development: Leatherworking requires a selection of skills, such as pattern making, reducing, sewing, and finishing. Pursuing this pastime can aid you in creating and enhancing these abilities, which can be valuable in other areas of life.

Link with Tradition: Leatherworking is a standard craft that has been practiced for centuries. By discovering and exercising this ability, you can connect with the past and preserve this cultural heritage for future generations.

Business Opportunity: Leatherworking can also be a profitable hobby for you. You can transform your hobby into a profitable venture by developing and marketing your natural leather products.

Customization: Leatherworking permits you to create customized items that fit your style and needs. You can choose the natural leather type, color, and layout to make distinctive things that mirror your character.

Therapeutic: Leatherworking can be a restorative and introspective activity. The emphasis, as well as the concentration required for leatherworking, can help in reducing tension as well as anxiousness, as well as enhance psychological clearness.

Social Connections: Taking part in leatherworking courses or attending leatherworking occasions can supply possibilities for social interaction and an area structure. You'll be able to find people who share your interest in this craft.

Upcycling: Leatherworking offers a terrific opportunity for upcycling old leather products. You can repurpose natural leather garments, bags, and footwear into new and useful products, minimizing waste and advertising sustainability.

Top 3 Beginner Mistakes

1 - Buying the pre-assembled toolkits.

These tools are often low quality, bent, and broken after a few days of use. Usually, these kits need better-quality tools and tools you don't need. Therefore, the key initially is having fewer but high-quality tools.

2 - Getting leather when you have yet to have a project in mind.

When buying leather from any reputed shops in your area, please ask the salesperson about the best-suited leather for your project.

3 - Making the process more complex

I see a lot of beginners getting caught up in buying lots of creams and power devices for finishing the leatherwork. The charm of typical leatherwork is that you're utilizing standard hand tools and techniques that have existed since simpler times! So, you can maintain it easily and also enjoy it.

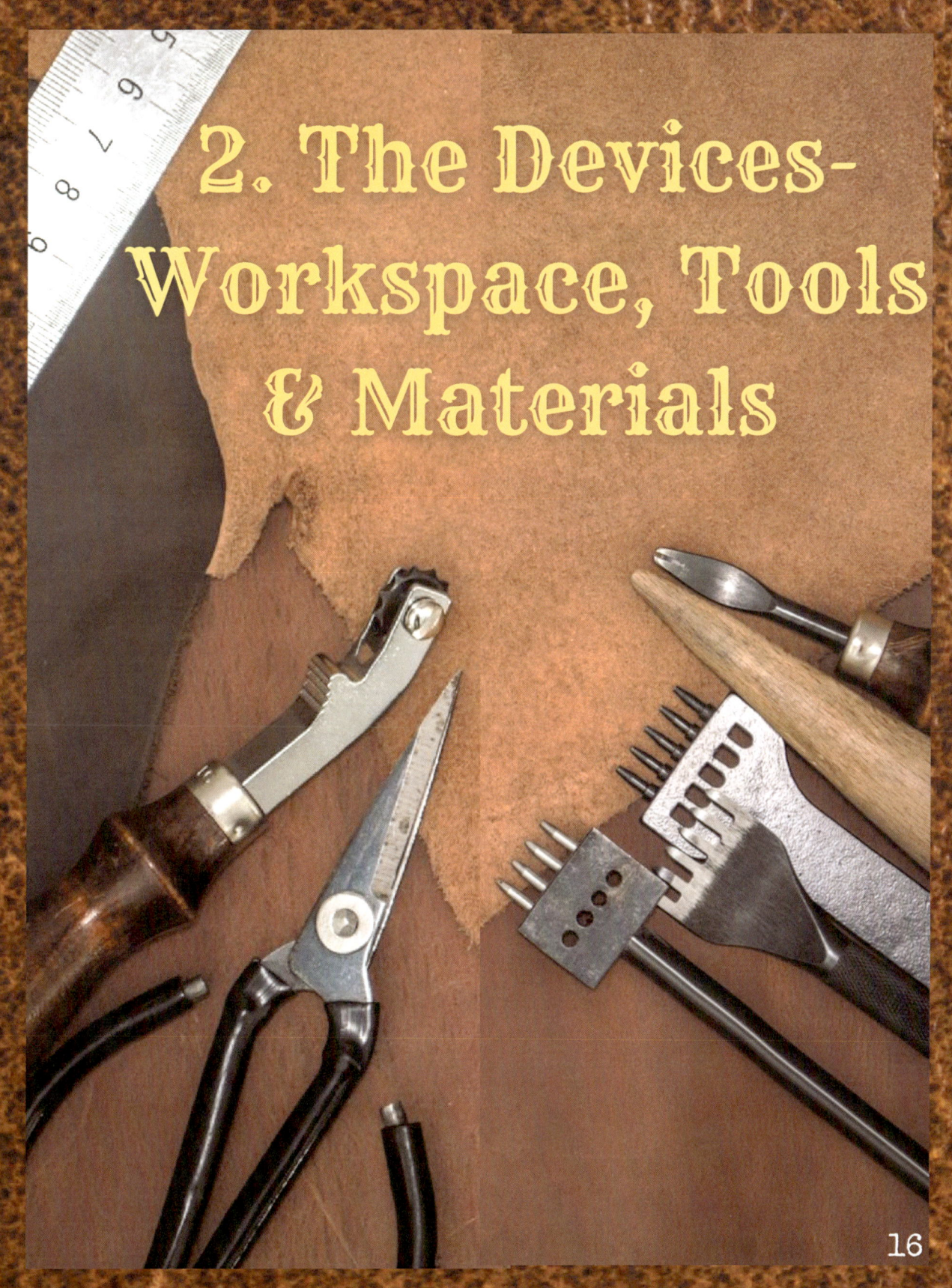

2. The Devices- Workspace, Tools & Materials

Setting Up an Ideal Workspace

There are 2 extremely crucial things to think about when establishing the Leathercraft workplace:

1. See to it that the working area is well-lit. A great configuration is overhanging fluorescent lighting combined with clamp-on, swing-arm fixtures that can be positioned over the project.

2. Ensure the area is well-ventilated. The dyes, cement, and finishes utilized in leatherworking might produce solid, hazardous fumes.

3. You will certainly likewise require a tough table or workbench to be used as a
- Design and assembly area
- Cutting space
- Carving and also stamping area
- Dyeing, staining, and also finishing location

Types of Tools

Many tools made used in leatherworking have sharp cutting edges.

They can be organized into three significant classifications, depending upon just how they are used :

- Tools that are **pushed** - ex: edgers, gouges, skivers, and some knives).
- Tools that are **pulled** - ex: swivel knives, utility blades, Groovers, and strap cutters).
- Tools that are **struck** - ex: punches and knives.

Make sure your devices are sharp-- a dull cutting device is dangerous. Grip them firmly to make complete control.

Never put any part of your body in the course of a cutting edge.

(A) Cutting Tools

1. Utility Knife - It is used to Cut leather with precision.

2. Rotary Cutter/Cutting Wheel - This knife comes with a little circular blade which rotates and cuts in straight line.

3. Round Knife- This knife has got a semicircular edge and is used for sophiticated cuts

4. Scissors- Most basic cutting tools used for cutting raw leather, thread and anything else.

5. X-Acto Knife - My favorite knife used for cutting any pattern into leather.

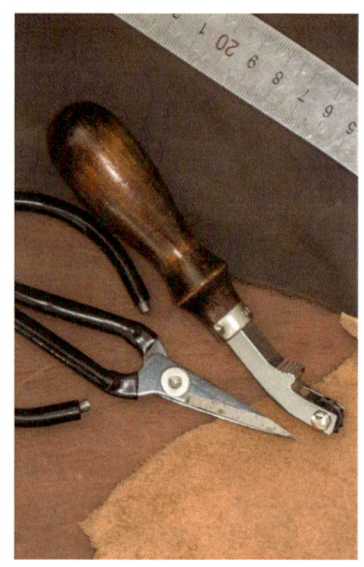
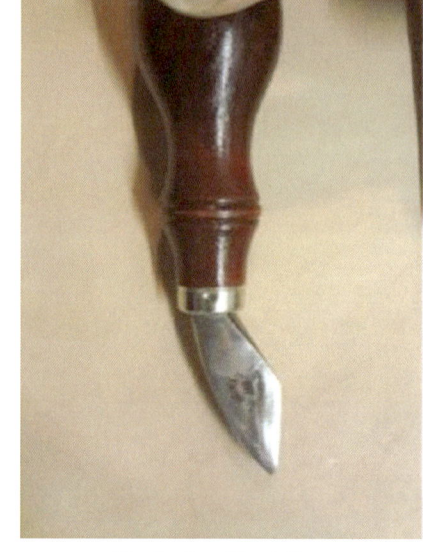
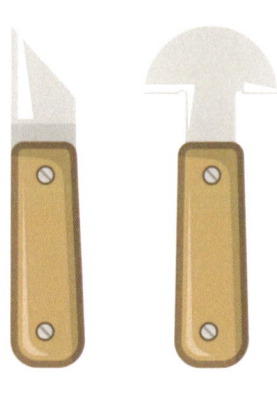

Scissor & Rotary Cutter   X-Acto Knife   Utility and Round Knife

Cutting Wheel

X-Acto Knife

Round Knife

(B) Punching/Hole Making Tools

1. **Hole Punch** - If you need to make hole in leather for sewing or lacing ,use this punch and strike it with a hammer gently.

2. **Stitching Chisel** - This is a tool with equally spaced teeth to make holes in a leather.

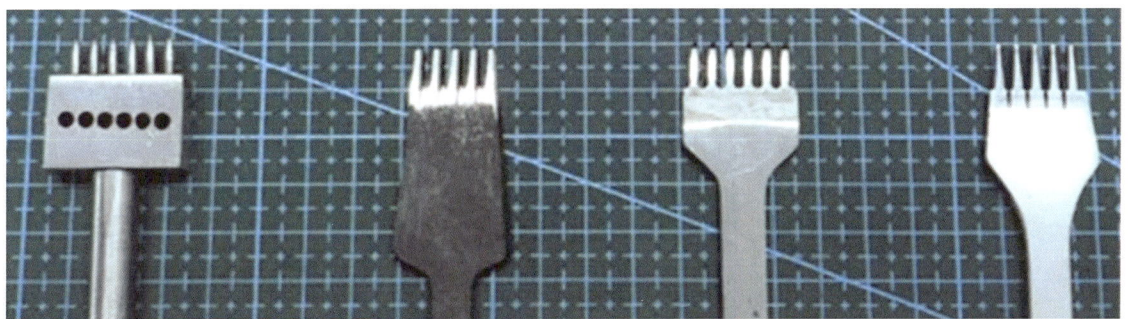

Round Punch Chisel   Crimson Iron   Diamond Chisel   Pricking Iron

3. **Pricking Iron** - Similar tool is pricking iron (flat teeth)but it only makes mark for making hole later on with an awl.

4. **Crimson Iron** (Japanese Style)- Its something between pricking iron and diamond chisel.It leaves a small hole when used as a chisel.

5. **Round Punch Chisel** - It makes a half mm round holes and used for basic stitching.

(C) Sewing Tools

1. **Needle** - It is used for hand sewing the leather piece.

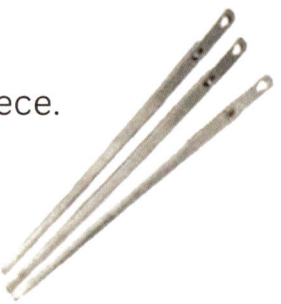

2. **Awl** - Multipurpose tool used for stitching & punching holes.

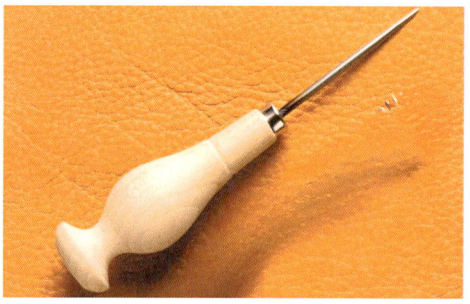

3. **Groover** - Before stitching it is used to make groove along the edges.

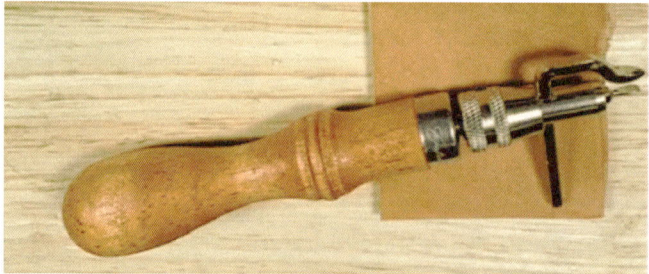

4. **Stiching Pony** - This tool holds the leather piece still while stitching.

(D) Edging

1. **Edge Beveler** - It makes the edge finish smooth & curve.

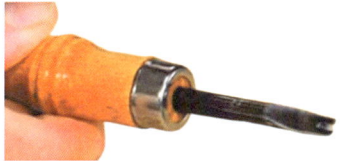

2. **Burnisher** - This wooden burnished is used after edge beveler and beveling polish to make the edge more smooth and polished.

(E) STAMPING/EMBOSSING

1. **Leather Stamps** - Used for imprinting a stamp design on leather.

2. **Heat Embosser**: Imprinting design through heat embossing.

 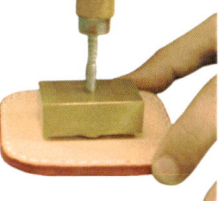

3. **Mallet** - Used to hit leather stamp for imprinting designs.

(F) Dying & Finishing

1. **Leather Dye** - It is used for coloring leather piece. I use lamb's wool to carry out dyeing.

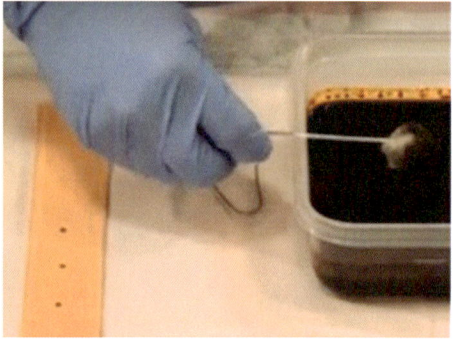 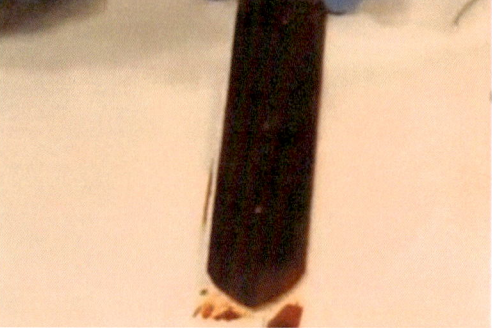

2. **Sponge** - It is used for applying color/dye on the leather piece.

3. **Conditioner** - It is used to soften the leather to prevent crack or drying.

4. **Sealer**: It is applied to save the leather from moisture and other environmental factors.

(G) Others /Misc.

1. **Skiving Knife(Skiving)** -It is used for make the thicker leather bit thinnerto fold and stitch it.

2. **V-Gouge(Folding)** - ·If you need to make a fold in leather, you use a straight edge to make a straight cut on the back side of the leather.

3. **Rivets (Hardware)** - Rivets allow you to attach two or even more pieces of natural leather together when they are connected with holes in the natural leather

4 .**Snaps(Hardware)**-Simple metal closures that are set into leather much like rivets. Snaps consist of four parts: the cap and the socket, and the post and the stud, and each pair is attached using a specialized setting tool.

5. **Swivel Knife (Design Carving)**- This knife is used to do intricate cuts with ease.

6. **Wing Divider (Marking)** - Used for marking precise distance from the edge of the leather piece .

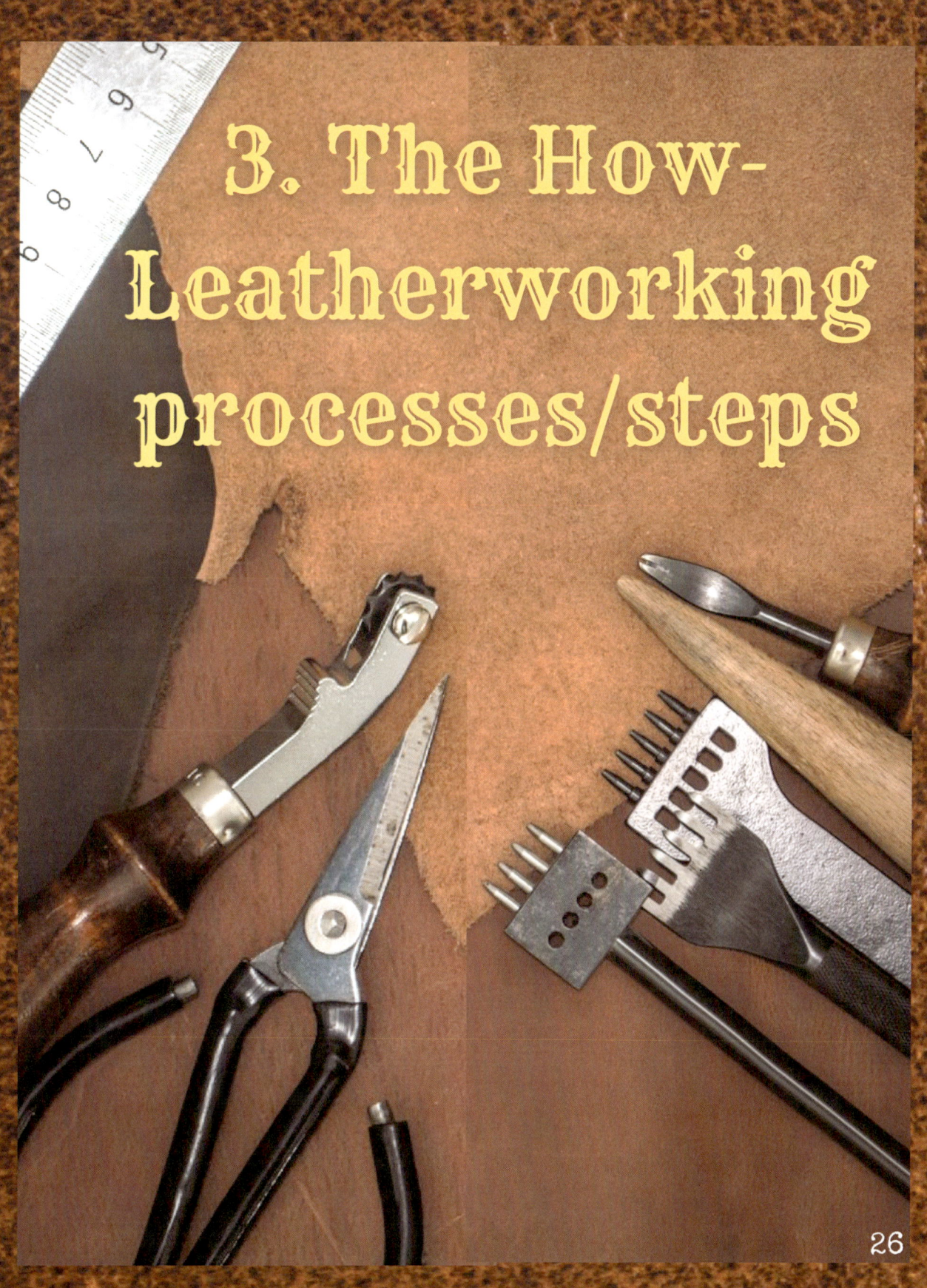

3. The How-Leatherworking processes/steps

Leatherworking Process Table

Process Name	What it does	Tools Used
Leather Selection & project preparation	Choosing right leather as per your project requirement	cutting mat, ruler, basic knife % scissors
Pattern making	Tracing the project design on the leather piece	pattern paper, tracing wheel, pattern notcher, ruler
Cutting	After tracing the pattern, cut the leather in the desired shape	cutting knife, cutting mat, ruler, leather shears
Skiving	The process of making the leather bit thinner if folding is required in the design.	skiving knife, skiving machine, sandpaper, ruler
Gluing	Sticking the design cut pieces as per the design pattern.	contact cement, glue brush, glue pot, glue spreader
Marking	Before punching or stitching this process make marks beforehand.	marking pen, chalk, awl, scratch awl
Punching	The process of making holes on leather piece for stitching or putting snaps, rivets etc.	hole punch, rotary punch, diamond punch, chisel

Process Name	What it does	Tools Used
Stitching	The process of sewing pieces of leather using thread.	stitching awl, needles, thread, stitching pony
Edging	The process of smoothening the edges of the leather piece.	cutting mat, ruler, basic knife % scissors
Burnishing	making edges smooth & polished using burnisher and wax	wooden burnisher, burnishing wax
Snapping & Riveting	joining of leather piece by rivet and snap	rivet setter, rivets, anvil, hammer, snap setter, snaps, anvil, hammer
Stamping	It is a process of making a design on leather using stamp by hitting it with mallet.	Stamp, Mallet, Cutting Mat
Embossing	Embossing is the process by which the leather crafter can elevate a portion of a leather or make a raised pattern.	Embossing heat tool, stamp
Beveling	smoothening the edges as part of finishig	beveler, sandpaper, slicker, ruler

Process Name	What it does	Tools Used
Casing	Process of dampening leather before tooling, stamping, or embossing it.	Sponge or Spray Bottle, Damp Cloth, Casing Mallet
Tooling	The process of creating patterns/designs on leather.	swivel knives, bevellers, and background tools
Dyeing	Coloring the leather in the process of finishing.	leather dye, dye applicator, sponge, gloves
Conditioning	Prevent cracking of leather by applying conditioning.	leather conditioner, sponge, cloth, gloves
Polishing	Finishing step for providing shining to the finished product.	leather polish, brush, cloth, gloves

Making simple card holder -understanding processes

Marking & Cutting the pattern

Tools: Utility knife, ruler, cutting mat

Steps:

a. Mark the natural leather using the ruler.
b. Use the knife/scissor to cut the leather along the lines.
c. The cutting mat protects the surface area and the knife blade.

Hole punching

Tools: Hole punch, hammer, cutting mat

Steps:

a. Use the hole strike to make holes in the leather where required.
b. Use the cutting mat beneath the leather to safeguard the job surface area and the tool.
c. Use the hammer to punch the holes into the natural leather.

Edging & Burnishing

Tools: Edge beveler, sandpaper, leather burnisher, leather edge dye

Steps:

a. Use the edge beveler to remove the sharp edges of the leather.
b. Ten use sandpaper to smooth the edges and get rid of any roughness.
c. Use the leather edge dye to the edges of the leather to finish the look.
d. Apply a leather burnisher to smooth out the edges and provide a refined surface.

Making simple card holder -understanding processes

Assembly

Tools: Needles, waxed string, leather glue, edge clamp

Steps:

a. Apply natural leather glue to assemble the leather pieces as per design.
b. Use the edge clamp to hold the pieces in position while the adhesive dries.
c. Use needles and waxed string to sew the assembled card holder.\

Finishing

Tools: Natural leather conditioner, cloth, polish

Steps:

a. Apply natural leather conditioner to the cardholder to keep the leather soft.
b. Use a soft cloth to rub the leather and offer it a polished coating.

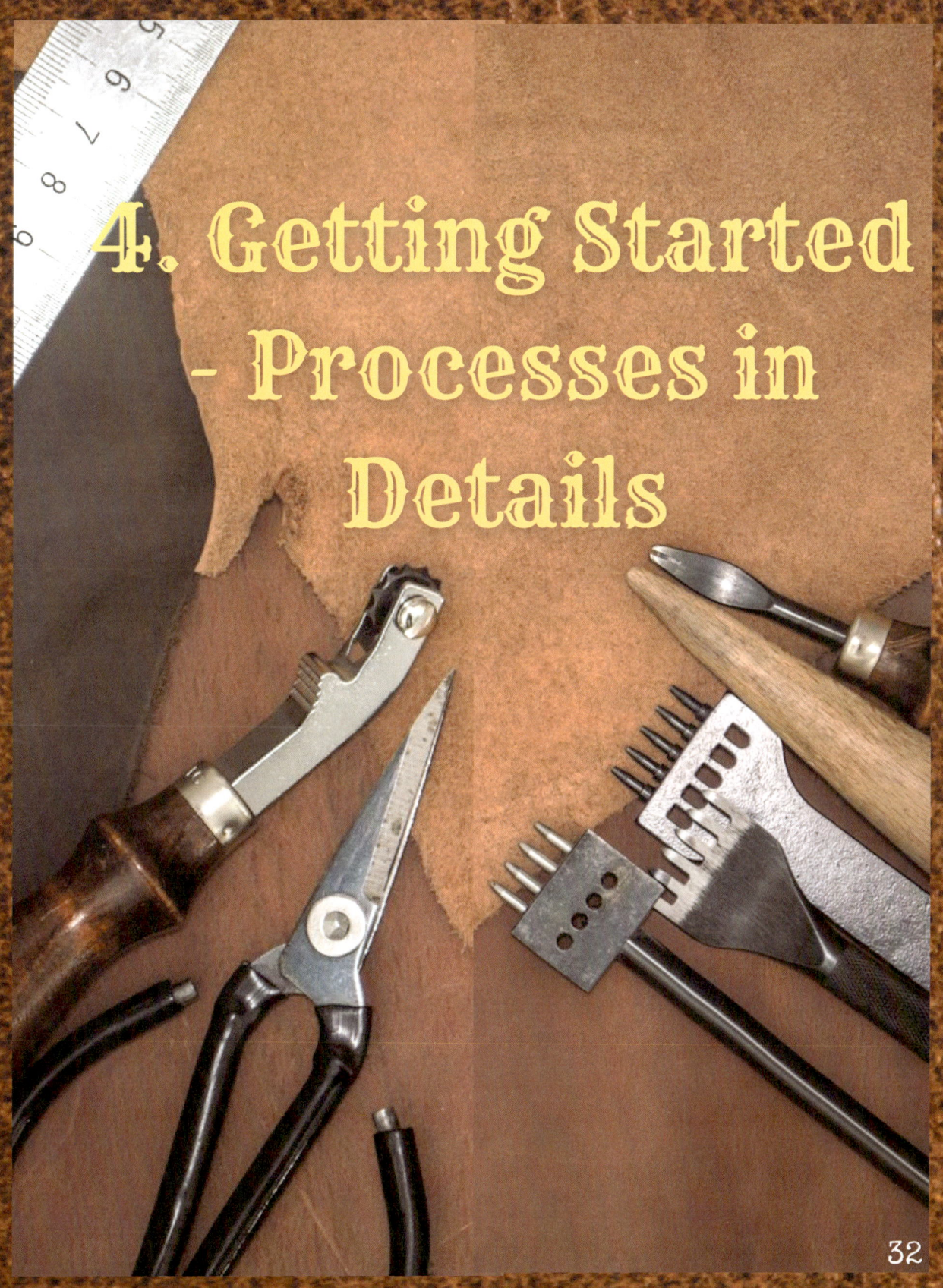

4. Getting Started - Processes in Details

In the last chapter, we understood the processes of leatherworking. In this chapter, we will discuss in detail a few strategies and tools which I feel you need to understand for your first project, which will be covered in the next chapter.

1. Drawing Patterns/Designs & Cutting

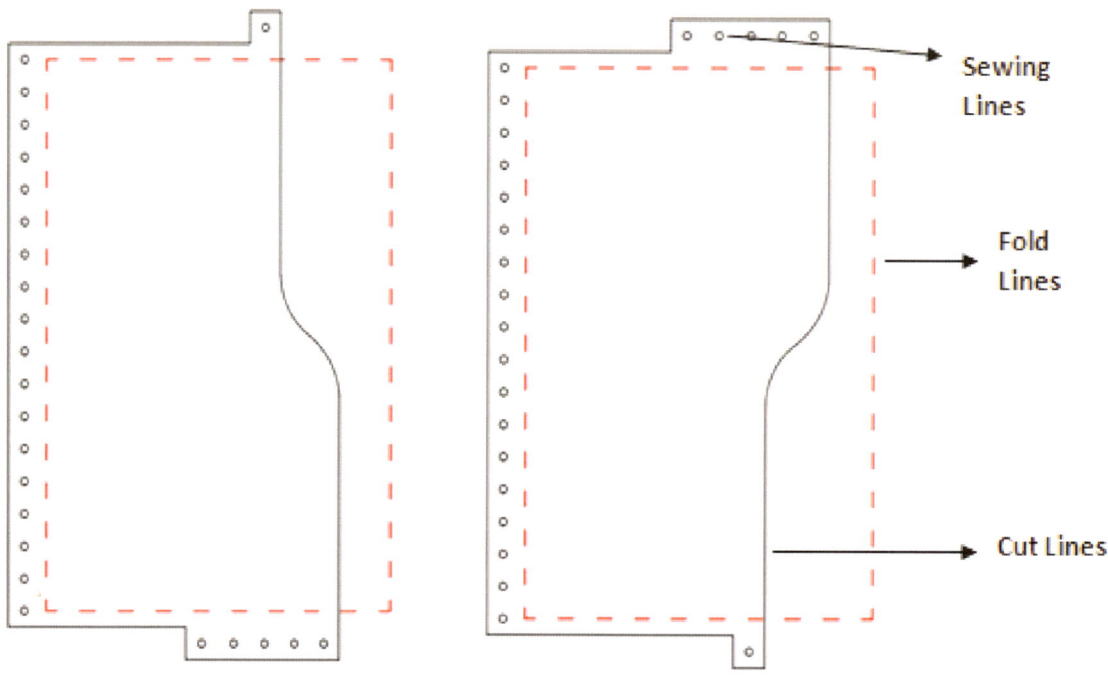

Patternmaking can be very technical when you're making patterns for intricate shapes.

A pattern is a two-dimensional layout that has all the information you need to cut certain forms out of a flat material that can be put together to create a design.

Wallet Pattern

Pattern Transfer onto cardboard template

Step 1— Draw/Print the pattern on paper keeping in mind all the holes & slits.

Step 2—Next step, make a cardboard template of each part by gluing the paper pattern of each part onto the cardboard with rubber cement or paper glue.

Step 3—Lastly, cut out each part of the cardboard, as per the paper patterns

Leather Cutting

Step 1— Place the leather on the cutting board with smooth side of the leather should kept up.(facing you)

Step 2—Next keep the templates on the leather so there will be little or no waste.

.

Step 3— Draw/Print the pattern on paper keeping in mind all the holes & slits.

Step 4—Hold each template firmly and draw its outline into the leather with a scratch awl.

Step 5—Lastly, Carefully cut out each part with a leather knife. Try to cut through the leather with a single stroke; the cut edge of the leather will be cleaner and neater if you don't have to go over it again. Use a ruler as a guide for the knife on straight cuts.

2. Punching Holes

Step 1: We can use a 1/16-inch hole punch to punch all stitching holes marked on the pattern. Also, leather should always be dry before punching holes.

Step 2: To create the slot for the strap, use a 1/8-inch hole punch to make a hole at each end of the slot position. Then use a blade to cut out the natural leather in between the holes to develop the slot. Next, use a rubber or poly board under the leather for drive punches.

Punching Tools

3. Design Transfer

Casing (Leather preparation before pattern transfer)

Preparing the leather Before you can move, you should dampen the leather after carving or stamping a style on the leather.

A sharp swivel knife blade will cut conveniently and efficiently, and stamping devices will imprint clearly and firmly into the leather only when the leather has been dampened (cased) to the appropriate level.

Understanding just how damp a piece of leather requires to be to reach this level comes with practice and individual choice.

Step 1- Wet the leather by casing it, massage a moist sponge on the flesh side of the leather as evenly as feasible. After that, turn the leather over and dampen the grain side (carving surface).

Step 2- When the moistened grain side of the leather has practically returned to its initial shade, it is ready to carve.

Design Transfer

Step 1- Whether you pick to carve or stamp the leather, it is easier if you initially draw the design using tracing paper and pen. After casing as the leather color returns to its usual self, it's time to transfer the design.

Step 2- Use a stylus pen to trace carefully, as shown in the photo below. Before removing the tracing paper, ensure the design has been appropriately transferred.

4. Decorating Leather(Tooling) - Various Tools & Processes

Carving the Leather

After the design transfer, we have to carve it, and here swivel knife is a very critical tool. So one thing you must do is practice a lot on leather scrap with a **swivel knife**. It is utilized to cut the main outline of the design as well as place decorative cuts in the item.

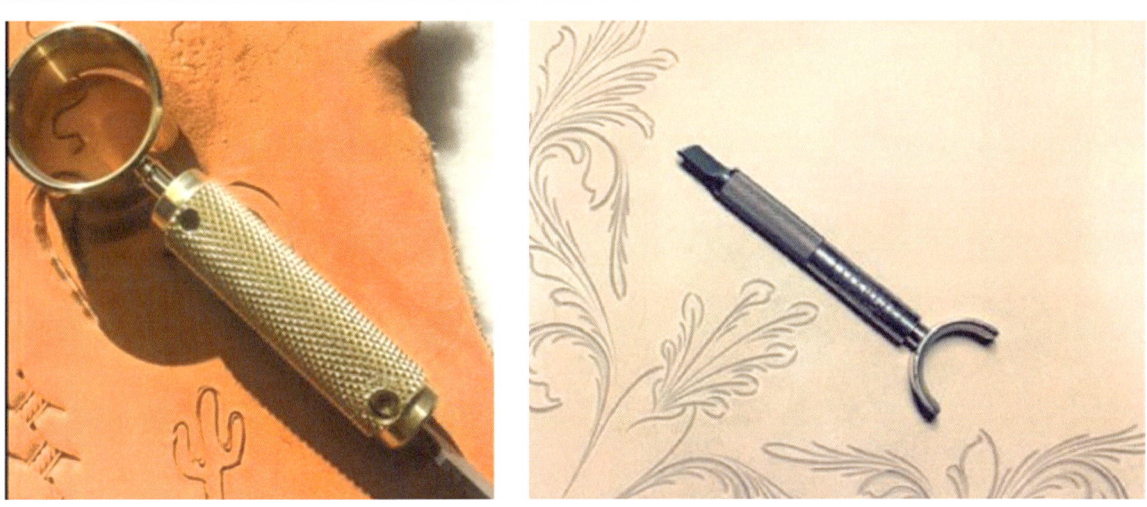

Camouflage

The next thing to do is use camouflage tools. It generates a texture effect. You have to hold it straight and use a mallet to strike it to produce an effect.

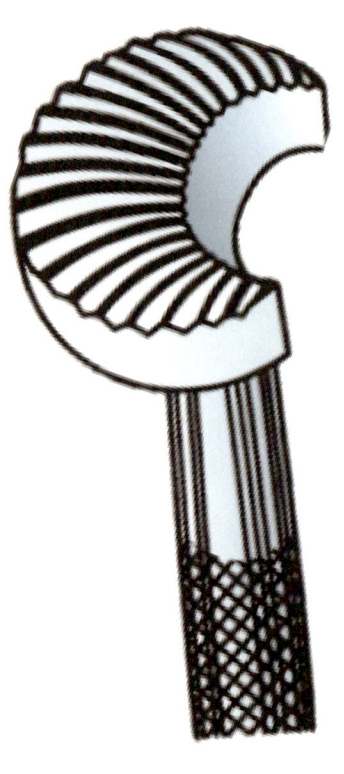

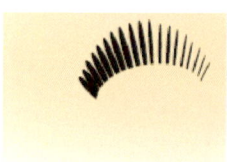
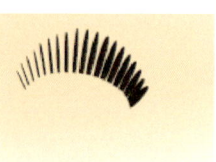

FULL IMPRESSION **LEFT-CORNER IMPRESSION** **RIGHT-CORNER IMPRESSION** **TOE IMPRESSION**

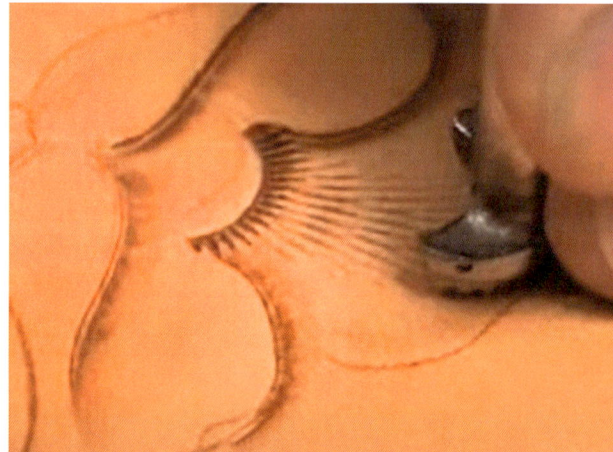
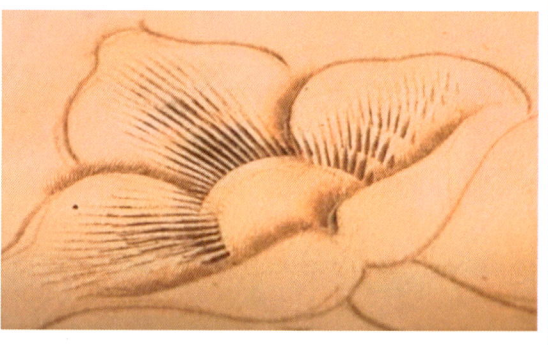

Pear Shader

The pear shader shapes the areas described by the swivel blade. It produces low spots and high spots for an extra all-natural look to the layout. Hold it straight up and down, and practice "walking" the pear shader. Use a jackhammer for strokes as you move the device slowly.

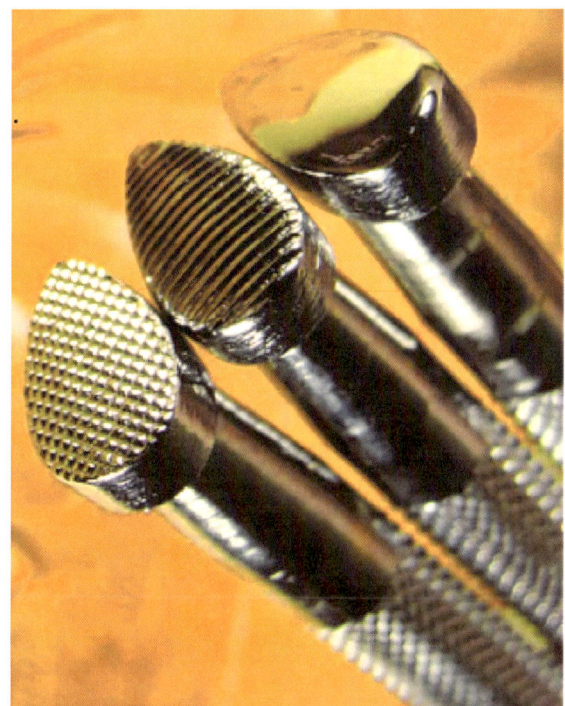
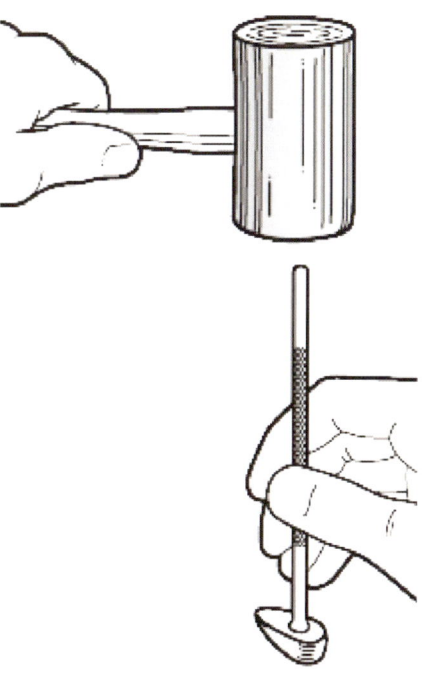
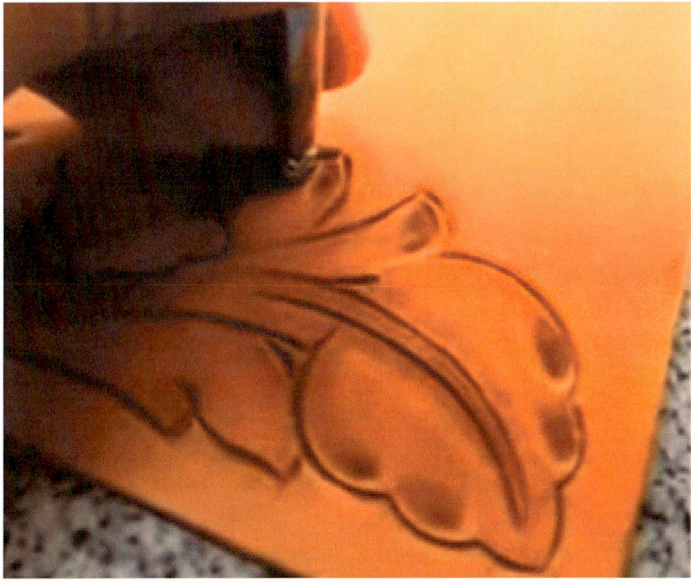

Beveler

The beveler is an additional "walking" tool utilized to lower the locations around the layout so that the style appears raised. Areas within the design are likewise beveled to develop an overlapping result from one part of the style to another. The toe of the beveler adheres to the lines made by the swivel knife.

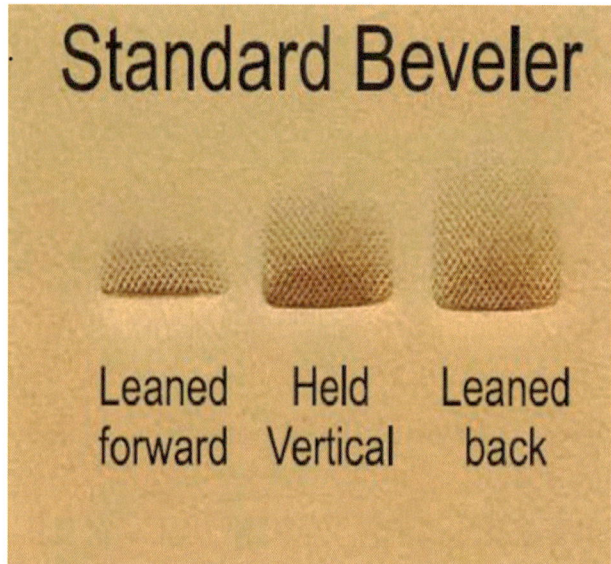

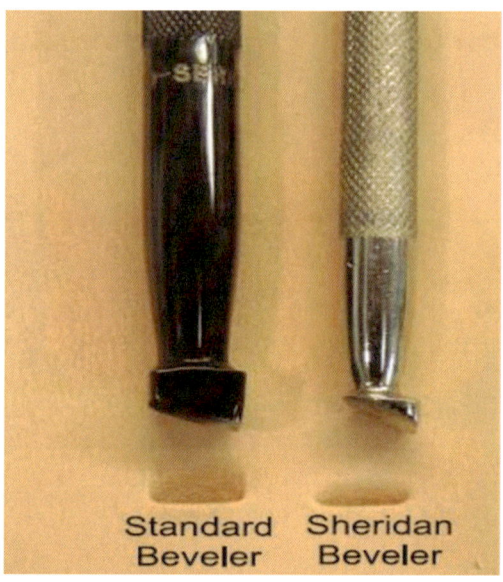

Veiner

The veiner is used to add veins to leaves and for various other special effects. Like the camouflage, the veiner is commonly leaned to one side or the other. The device's angle identifies the impact's length and makes it fade out as it goes away from the swivel cut.

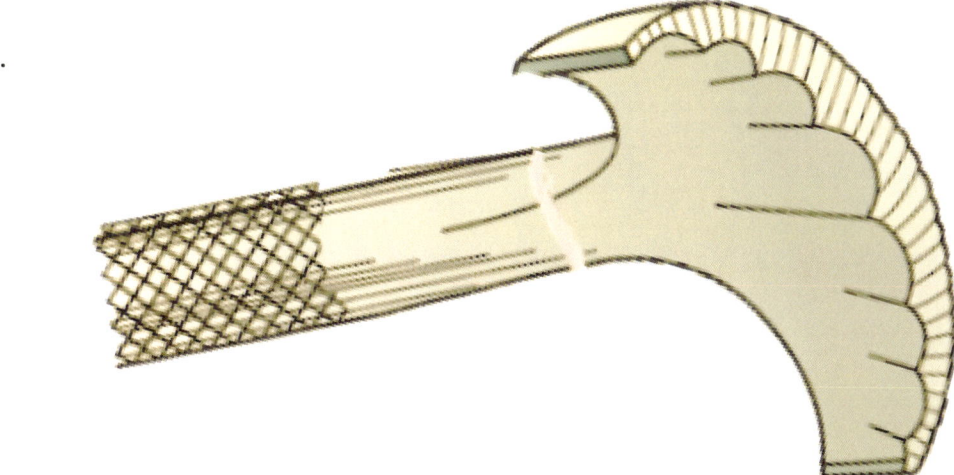

Seeder

The seeder is used for making seed pods in the leather design. This tool is much smaller than the others, and also it does not take virtually as much pressure to make a deep perception in the leather.

The external row of seeds is marked first, and after that, the second row, and more until the pod location is made.

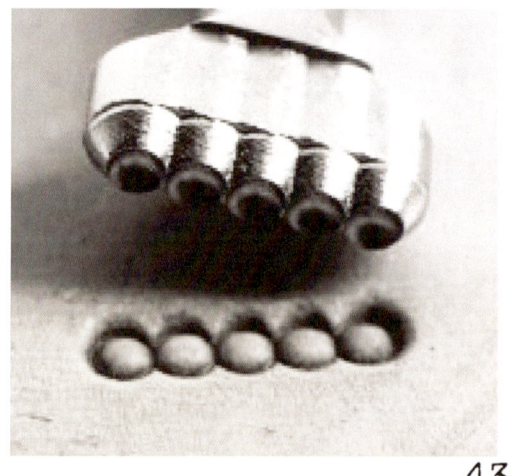

Backgrounder

The backgrounder pushes the background within and around the design to make it look distinct from the carving.

Hold the tool straight and down and try to make each impression the same depth.

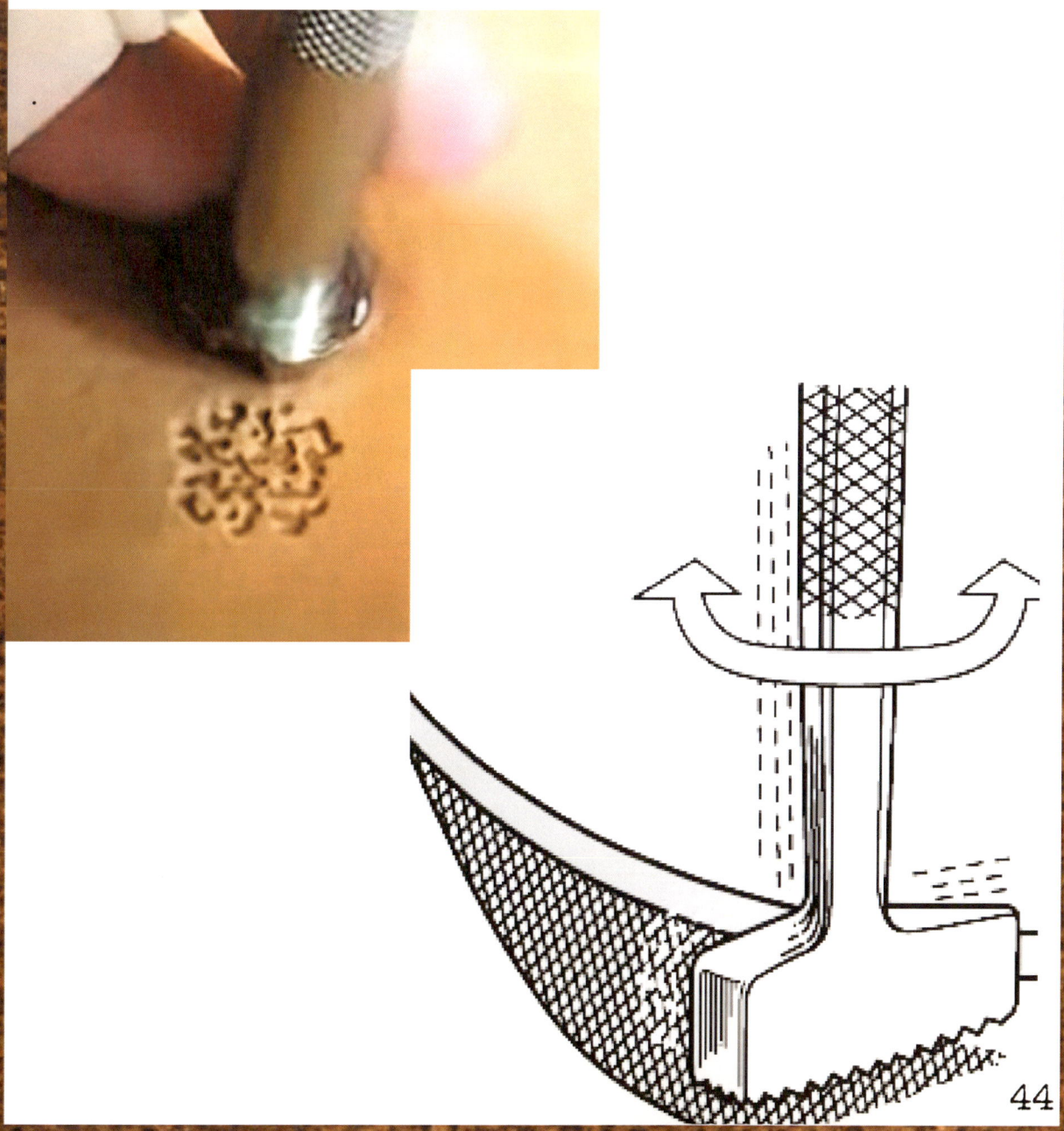

5. Stitching

Leather stitching is a crucial skill for any leather crafter. It is the procedure of joining two or more pieces of leather with each other with the help of a needle and string.

There are numerous types of stitching in leather crafting. Every kind of stitching solves specific purposes and also has its one-of-a-kind look.

Below are several of one of the most common kinds of stitching:

Single Stitch :

 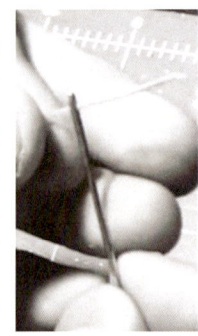 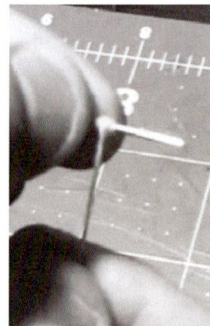 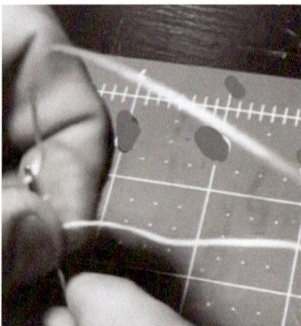

Use groover to make stitching lines & then holes on those lines for stitching

Insert thread into needle eye. Make other end of thread several rounds around needle and pull it upside to make a knot.

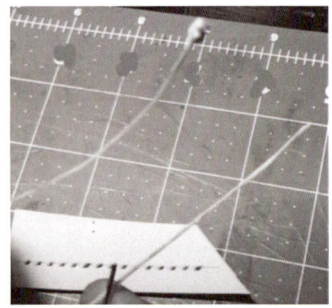 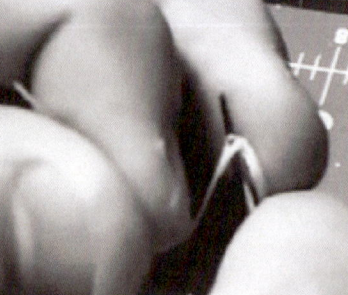 

Insert the needle into a thread of the other end as shown, and pull it to make another knot.
The stitch should be in 2 forward and 1 backward style.

45

Single stitch in a leather purse

Z Stitch :

Insert the thread into the needle eye. Make the first knot at one end and the other end, as shown in the last stitch.

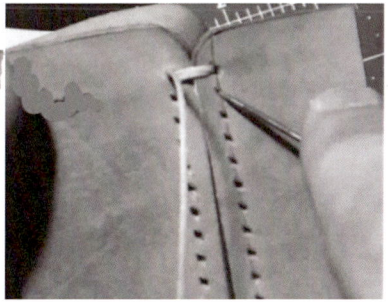

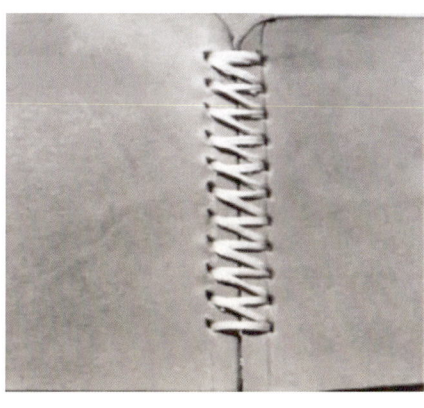

As shown in the picture, first make take the thread through needle in the adjacent hole and then to one below to give it Z shape

Cross Stitch :

Cross stitches are incredibly popular in leatherworking since they develop a very appealing criss-cross or X pattern where two pieces of natural leather join.

Each item of natural leather has equally spaced holes along its external edge. The string is, after that, woven back and forth in an X pattern, like just how you would certainly link the laces of your athletic shoe or sneakers. But, rather than a bow at the end, these stitches are connected off and melted in place if the thread is synthetic.

This type of stitch is one of the simplest leather stitches to find out, especially if you're seeking a slightly more decorative style than what the single stitch or straight stitches supply. Even better, these stitches are strong and durable and will undoubtedly last long wherever they are sewn.

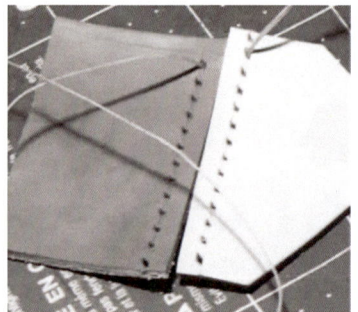

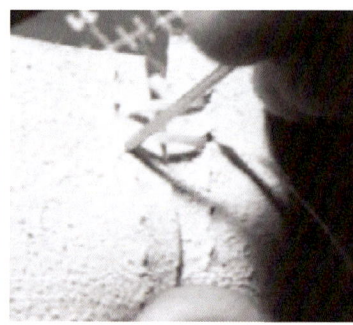

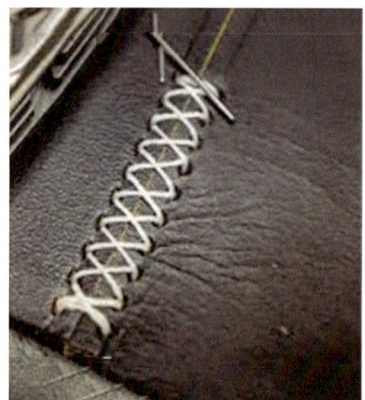

As shown in the picture, notice the cross stitches.

6. Finishing

The finishing procedure adds a safety layer to the surface of the leather.

It assists in preventing scrapes, water damage, as well as various other types of damage.

There are two primary sorts of finishes: safety and also decorative.

Protective finishes

They are made to keep the leather secure from the elements. They are usually clear as well as do not alter the shade of the leather. The most usual sorts of protective finishes are:

Resolene: This is a clear, water-based finish that dries out quickly and gives excellent protection against water and stains.

Acrylic: This is a clear, water-based finish that dries quickly as well as offers excellent defense against water and also stains.

Decorative finishes

These are created to add color or structure to the leather. They are readily available in a selection of colors and finishes, consisting of glossy, matte, and metal. The most usual types of decorative finishes are:

Satin Sheen: This finish is semi-glossy as well as includes a refined sheen to the leather.

High Gloss: This finish is very shiny and also reflective, making it a prominent choice for dress footwear as well as bags.

Antique: This finish includes a vintage or troubled aim to the leather.

Dyeing

Dyeing is the procedure of including shade in the leather. There are two primary types of dyes: water-based and also oil-based.

Water-based dyes are easy to use and supply a vast array of colors. They are also extra eco-friendly than oil-based dyes. The most usual sorts of water-based dyes are:

Fiebing's Pro Dye: This dye is simple to apply as well as gives a wide variety of shades. It additionally dries out promptly as well as generates a matte finish.

Angelus Leather Dye: This dye is popular amongst leather crafters because it generates dynamic colors and dries rapidly.

Oil-based dyes are harder to use yet generate much deeper, richer shades. They are likewise more resilient than water-based dyes. The most usual sorts of oil-based dyes are:

Fiebing's Oil Dye: This dye is easy to use as well as generates a rich, deep shade. It is also very sturdy and resistant to water as well as stains.

Eco-Flo Leather Dye: This dye is eco-friendly and produces a wide variety of shades.

Application

Applying finishes and dyes requires some practice; however, it is a basic procedure. Here are some pointers for applying finishes and also dyes:

Clean the leather: Prior to applying any type of finish or dye, make sure the leather is clean and also without any dust or particles.

Apply in thin layers: Use finishes and also dyes in thin coats to stay clear of unequal color or texture.

Make use of a sponge or brush: Use finishes as well as dyes utilizing a sponge or brush. This will certainly help to disperse the item equally and also prevent streaks.

Let it dry: Enable the leather to completely dry entirely between layers of finishes or dyes.

Buff the leather: After applying finishes or dyes, buff the leather with a soft towel to eliminate any kind of excess item and develop a smooth finish.

Finishing and dyeing your leather products can be an enjoyable and fulfilling experience. Bear in mind to pick the appropriate sort of finish or dye for your project, use it in slim coats, as well as permit the leather to dry totally completely. With method and perseverance, you can produce lovely leather items that will certainly last for many years to come.

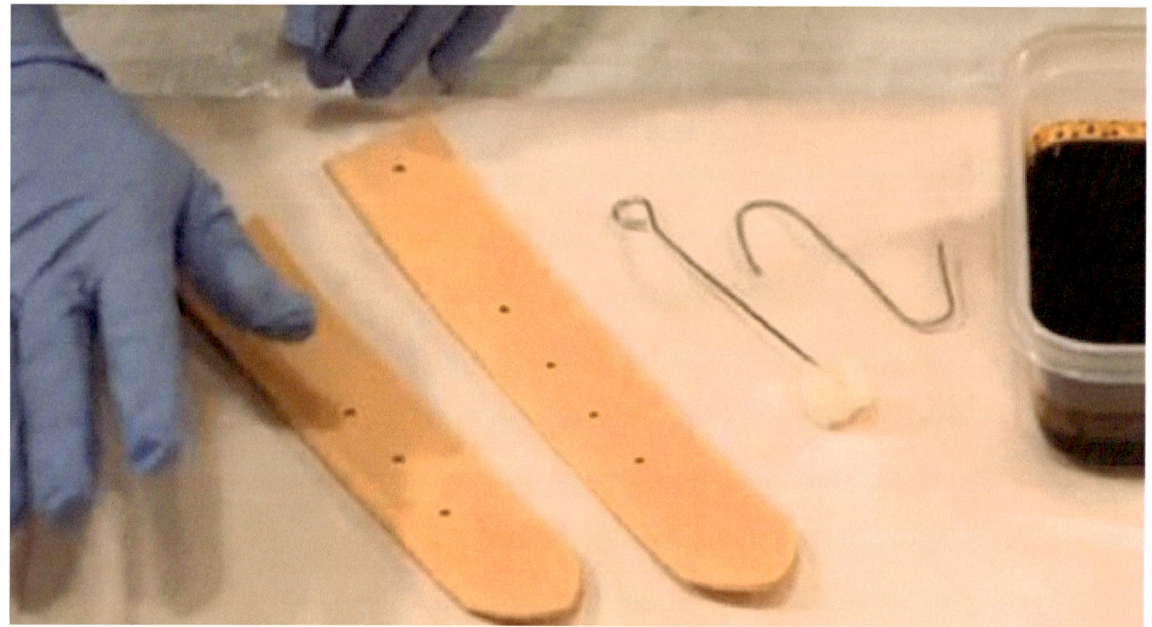

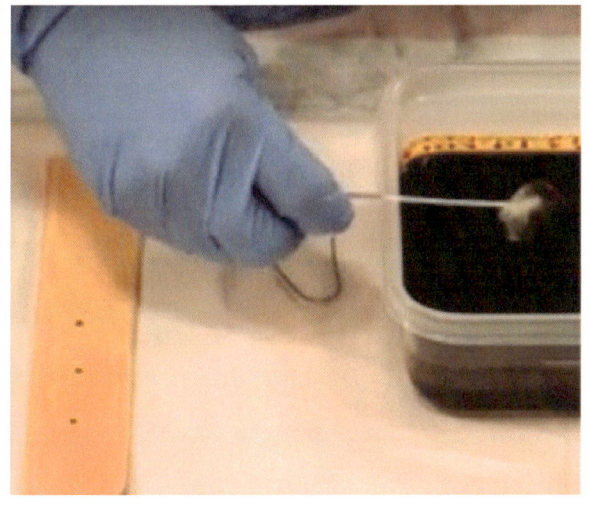 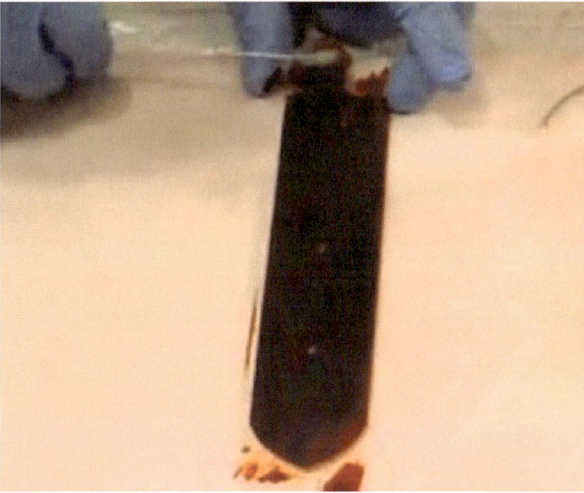

Dyeing using Lamb's Wool

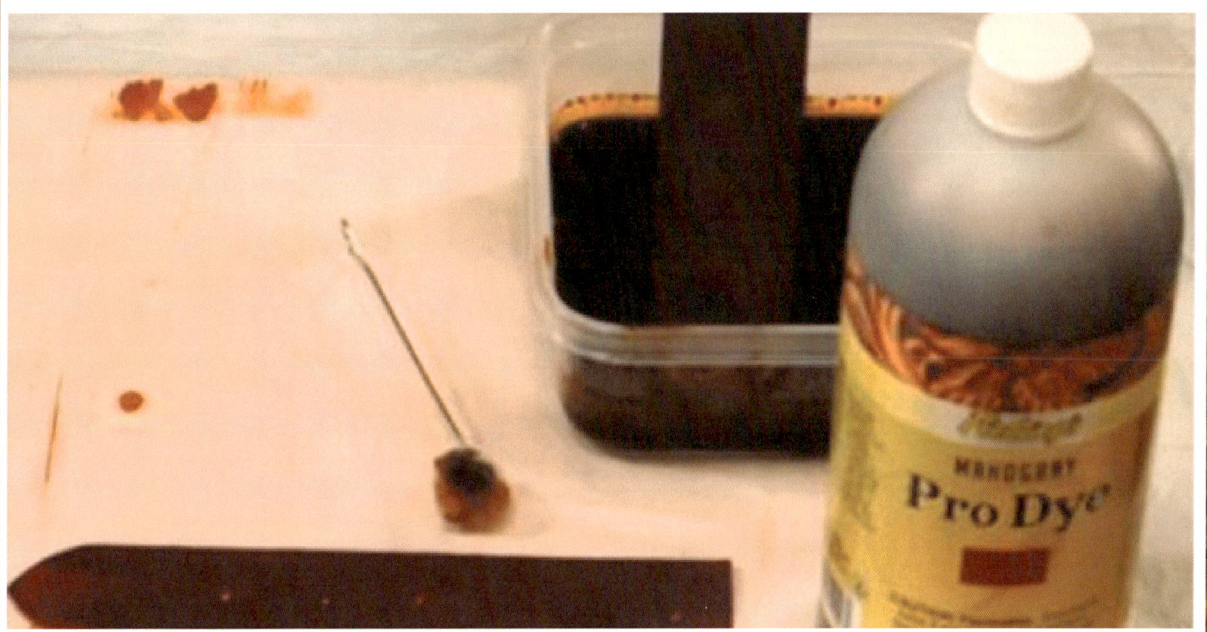

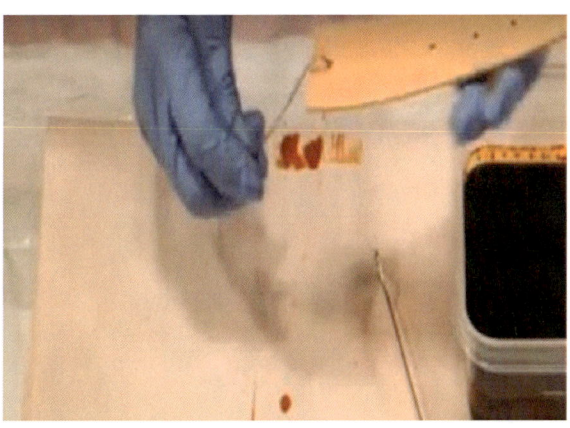

Dip Dye

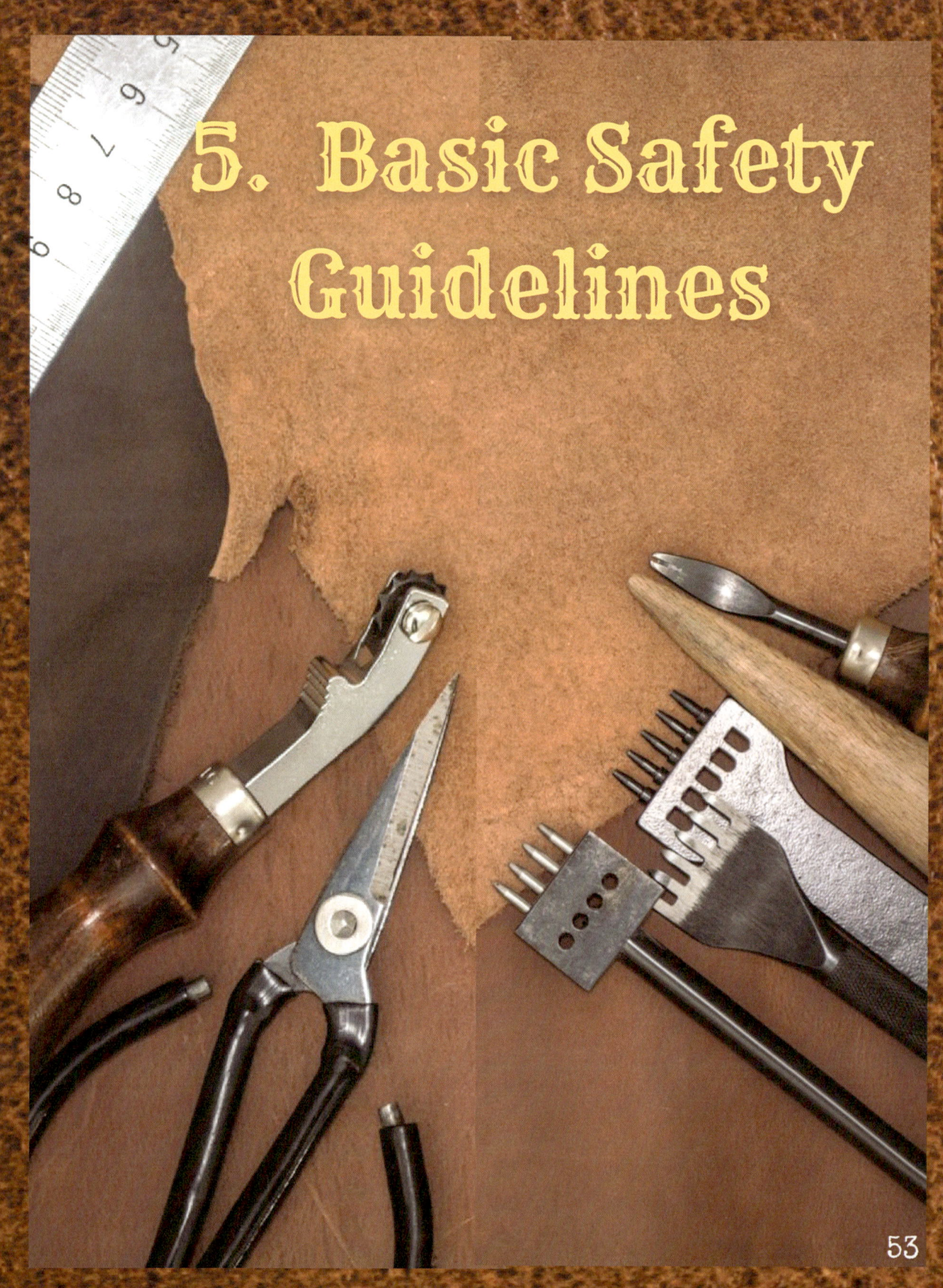

5. Basic Safety Guidelines

Safety and First Aid in Leatherworking

Many tools are used in leatherworking to safeguard against sharp edges and any untowardly incident.

The tools can be categorized into three categories as per their use:

- Tools that are pressed, like edgers, gouges, skivers, as well as some knives

Skiver   Adjustable V-Gouge   edger

- Tools that are pulled, like swivel knives, utility knives, groovers, as well as strap cutters

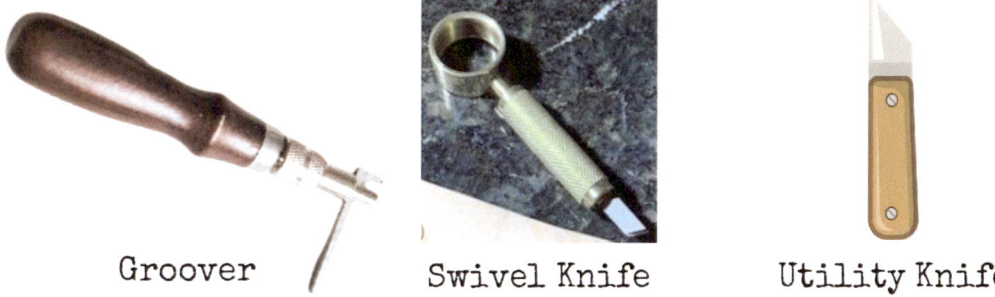

Groover   Swivel Knife   Utility Knife

- Tools that are struck like punch and chisels

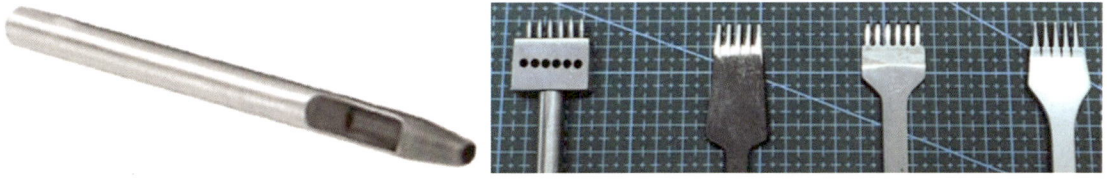

Tips :

- See that your tools are sharp-- a worn-out cutting tool is dangerous.

- Grip them firmly to guarantee complete control.

- Never place any part of your body on a cutting-edge path.

- Many dyes, cement, and coatings utilized in leatherworking include dangerous chemicals.

- To securely make use of these products, operate in a well-ventilated location.

- Thoroughly review and also adhere to all tag directions as well as cautions.

- Never ingest these chemicals or enable them to contact the skin.

- Shield your hands by putting on rubber gloves. Replace caps and also lids to prevent spills.

- Never make use of chemicals near an open fire. Instead, have a medical professional or emergency medical service phone number convenient in an emergency.

Cuts & Scratches

Cuts and scratches are wounds or openings in the skin and tissues that can permit germs to go into the body and cause infection.

Puncture wounds can be hazardous because they allow germs right into an injury that is tough to clean.

Remember, any individual enduring a major wound must be treated for shock and also seen by a physician immediately.

Steps of treatment :

For minor scratches and cuts:

- Clean the injury with soap as well as water.
- Apply disinfectant to help prevent infection.
- Keep the injury clean by covering it with an adhesive bandage.

For larger cuts:

- Apply direct stress to control bleeding.
- clean the injury to avoid infection.
- Cover the open wound with a sterile gauze pad or clean towel folded right into a pad.

For puncture wounds:

- Let the wound bleed so that any particle which went inside comes out.
- Wash the place with soap and water, use a sterilized bandage, and see a physician.

Skin Inflammation

Some dyes, cement, and finishes may trigger redness, a burning experience, itching, or swelling if they enter contact with the skin.

How to treat:

- Clean the affected area with soap and also water.
- Seek medical focus quickly if the irritation continues

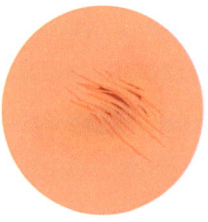

Consumed Poisoning

Poisoning is the most common reason for accidental fatality among young children. They will eat virtually anything, including the chemicals used in leatherworking, so keep such materials out of their reach.

Signs of poisoning include nausea or vomiting, stomach pains, burns around the mouth, and irregular breathing.

The most crucial indicator of poisoning is the presence of the toxin-- open bottles, spilled chemicals, or other proofs of what is being consumed by the kid.

How to treat:

- Right away, find a telephone, take any poisonous substance containers you see along with you, and call the poison control center of the neighborhood.
-Call the nearest doctor.
- Only offer something by mouth if you are told to do so by medical professionals.

Best Practices for Beginners

- Use protective gear like gloves, eye goggles, and masks when working with chemicals and devices.

- Maintain your work area clean and also organized to avoid mishaps.

- Use sharp blades and tools to stay safe from cuts or scratches after applying pressure.

- Always cut away from your body and ensure your fingers are out of the way.

- You can use a cutting mat to avoid damage to your work surface and keep your blades sharp.

- When using a swivel knife, constantly cut at a 45-degree angle and use a cutting board to avoid damage to your blade.

- When stamping or tooling leather, utilize a mallet instead of a hammer to stop harmful your tools.

- Use the proper dimension as well as the weight of the hammer for every device to stay clear of damage and boost accuracy.

- Use a leather punch to make clean and exact holes in your natural leather.

- Use a leather burnisher to smooth and polish the sides of your natural leather after cutting.

- Use natural leather adhesive moderately and adhere to the manufacturer's guidelines.

- Utilize a leather conditioner to keep your leather flexible and also avoid splitting.

- Use a natural leather color or end up in a well-ventilated location to prevent breathing in fumes.

- Prevent utilizing sharp objects like scissors or knives to pry open stitches or joints, as it can harm your leather.

- Practice good ergonomics to stay clear of repetitive strain injuries. Take breaks regularly and also extend your hands and also wrists regularly.

- Use caution when utilizing a hammer or mallet. Ensure your fingers are free from the striking area and prevent the hard-hitting of your devices.

- Ensure ventilation when dealing with chemicals such as dyes or adhesives. Use a respirator if required and stay clear of breathing in fumes or vapors.

6. Let's Make Something - 10 Starter Projects

(1) Simple Keychain

Tools Required :

- Leather scraps
- Steel ruler
- knife
- awl
- needle
- pencil or pen
- waxed thread
- glue
- lighter
- paper clips/clamps

Steps :

- Cut a leather piece you got using your steel ruler with a leather cutting knife.

- The size of your leather piece depends on your choice. I made it using a leather piece of dimensions 225 x 20 mm.

- Now measure to mark as per the width of your leather strip, here 20 mm.

- Using your project knife, thin the end of the natural leather strip, then use some glue, fold the thinned area in half, and clamp to completely dry. After sometime once the glue is dry remove the clamp.

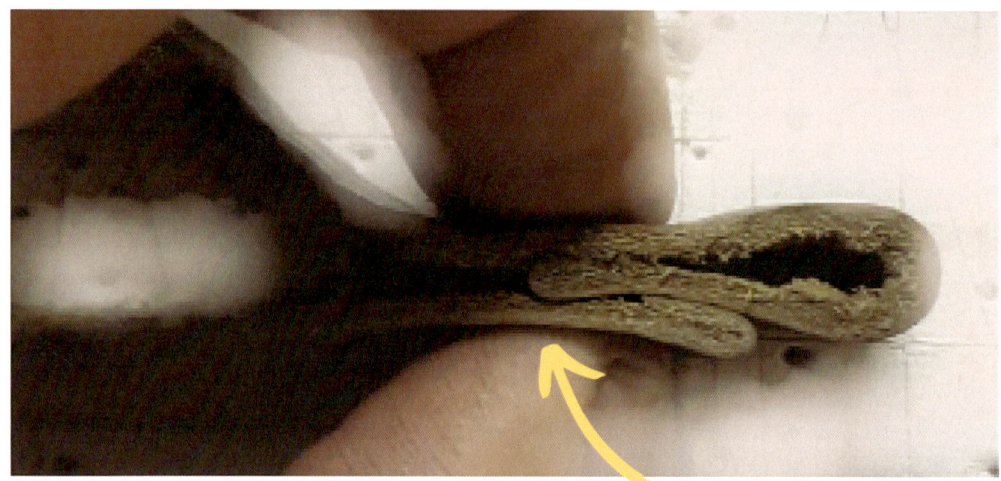

Make punch hole here

- Using awl punch holes, make 5 holes at the point shown above.

- Then use needle and thread to stitch in a square box with criss cross style as shown below.

- Dye the leather with Lamb's Wool and Dip Dyeing for making it shiny and of the desired color.

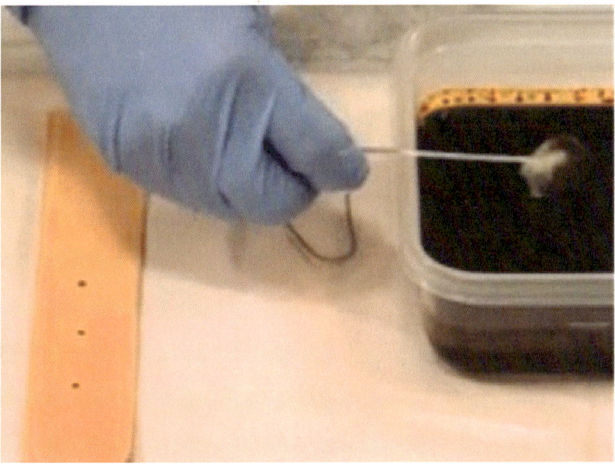 

- Dye the leather with Lamb's Wool and Dip Dyeing to make it shiny and of the desired color.

- After the dye is dried, apply polish of your choice to make the finish more glossy.

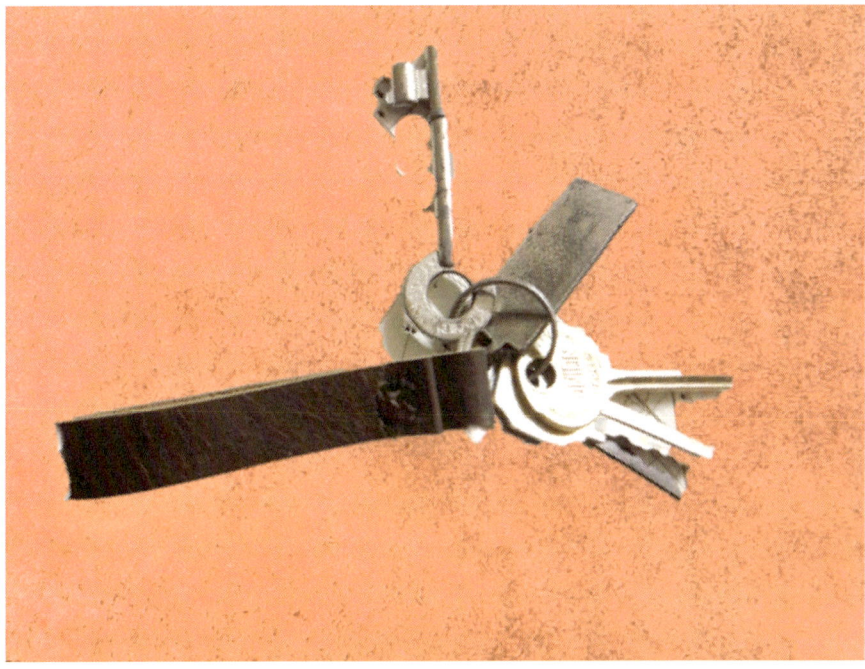

(2) Leather Bracelet out of Old Leather Belt

Tools Required :

- Old Leather Belt (about 9 inches off the end with holes in it)
- Steel ruler
- knife
- awl
- pencil or pen
- Cufflink (from old suit)
- Finishing items (as you like)- oil, waxing, acrylics, and synthetic waterproofing.

Steps :

- First, measure your wrist and mark the same on the end of the belt. Next, check your comfort level by keeping the belt around your wrist; it should be tight enough.

- Then make a hole with an awl or other punching tool. Punch a hole approximately 1/2 inch from the end of the belt edge, ensuring it does not have any other holes that would merge and make the hole large enough for the cufflink. Also, do not punch the hole too close to the edge, as the leather will stretch over time and possibly rip.

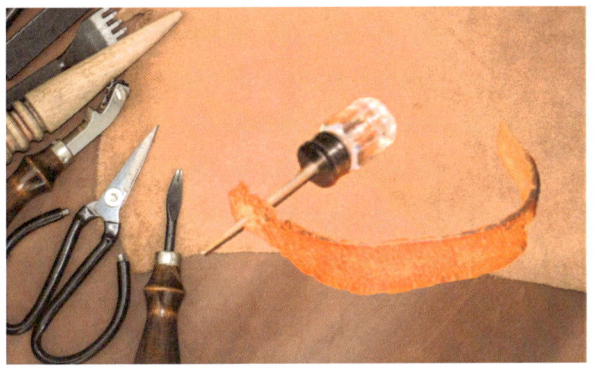 

- Then fix the cufflink in the hole with a flat edge facing your wrist.

- If you like, apply wax, oil, or dye to change the color and make it glossy. I liked the rugged look, so I avoided any finishing.

- You can also change the shape, use leather thread instead of cufflinks, and apply the design on the leather like the below design of the leather bracelet.

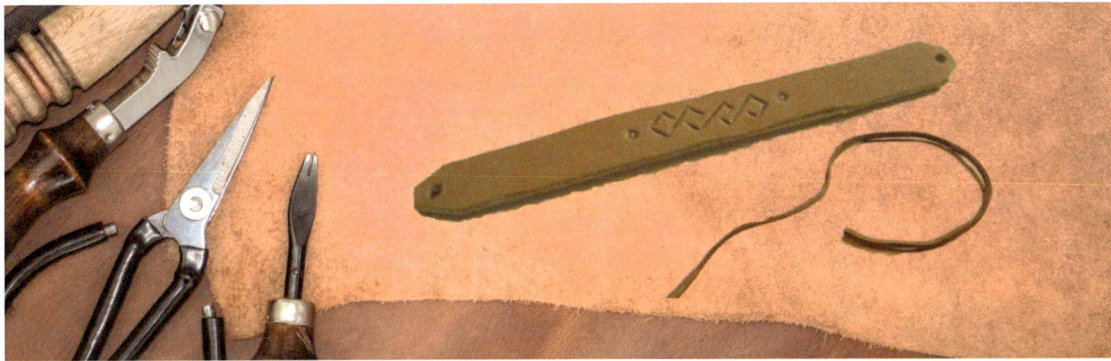

(3) Leather Coin Pouch

Tools Required :

- Leather piece (4 pieces from 4-5 inches of leftover leather)
- Steel ruler
- knife
- awl
- pencil or pen
- Needle & thread
- Finishing items (as you like)- oil, waxing, acrylics, and synthetic waterproofing.

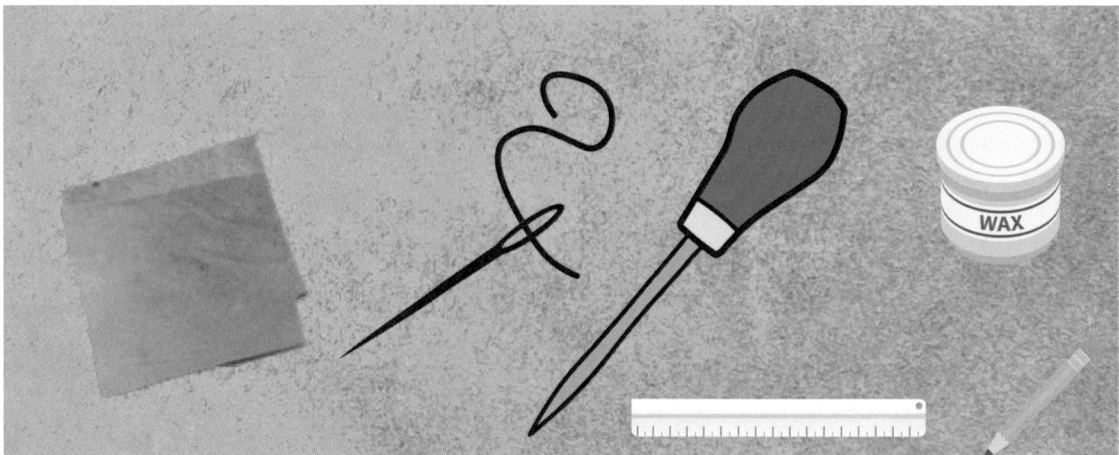

Steps :

- Cut the leather piece into 4 parts. The first 2 are identical & rectangular body parts. One flap and one for closure/locking. Refer to the photo below to understand more clearly.

- You can place all 4 pieces on the wooden block as you want to stitch them. Now create holes using an awl and hammer.

- Place them on a wooden board and create holes along the sides for stitching. Next, prepare your needle and thread for flat blanket stitches along the sides to attach the 2 body pieces and 1 closure piece. Finally, tie a knot and cut off extra thread.

- The remaining leather piece is the flap attached using a cross "x stitch, as shown below.

- Apply some finishing (wax in my case). Finally, your coin pouch is ready!

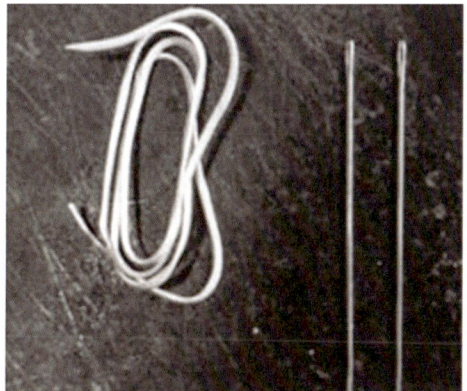

- You can also change the shape, use leather thread instead of cufflinks, and apply the design on the leather like the below design of the leather bracelet.

(4) Leather Pen Cover

Tools Required :

- Leather piece (rectangular shaped, length = pen cap length)
- Steel ruler
- knife
- awl
- pencil or pen
- Needle & thread
- Finishing items (as you like)- oil, waxing, acrylics, and synthetic waterproofing.

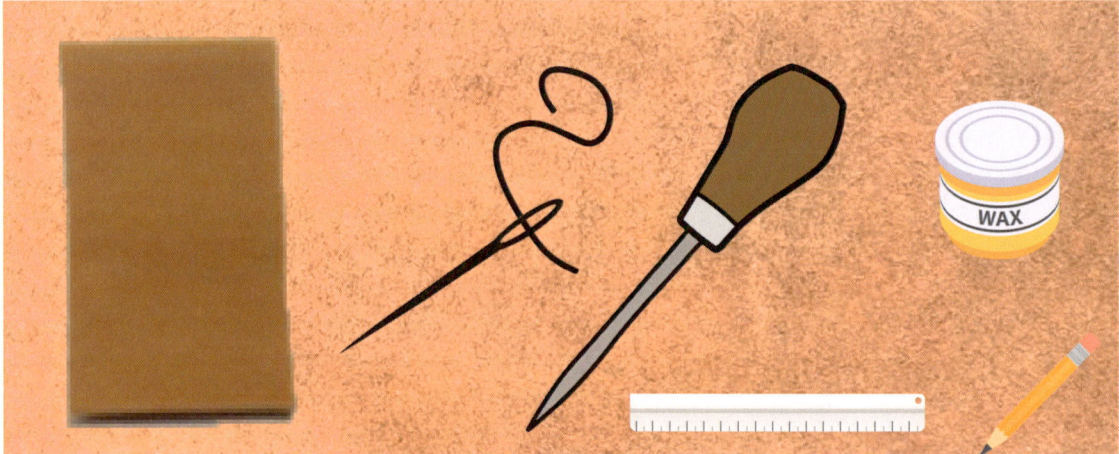

Steps :

- Keep your pen on the leather piece and then fold the leather till both ends meet/touch.

- Cut the piece per the pen's length and make a curve/scallop shape at the top, as shown in the figure below. Keep some extra leather at the ends for stitching.

- Now fold the leather and mark the area for stitching the ends.

- Use an awl or punch to make holes for stitching.

- Use the flat blanket stitching method to stitch it at one go from one end to the other. Cut the extra thread after tying a knot at the end.

- Apply wax to make it shine.

(5) Leather Passport Cover

Tools Required :

- Leather
- Ruler
- Utility Knife
- Head Screw Driver
- Hammer
- Contact Cement
- Nail
- Two Needles
- Waxed Thread
- Sandpaper
- Leather Polish (Optional)

Standard Passport Size

Steps :

- Get a leather piece. The standard size of a passport, as per international aviation standards, is 4.921×3.465 inches.

- Cut the leather piece as per below & cut using a metal ruler for a straight cut.
    - 1 piece-Body cover: 8.07 x5.61 inches -rectangle shaped
    - 2 piece- Flaps of the cover: 2.36x5.61 inches

- The next step is gluing. Apply the glue along the edges of the main body and flaps. Then align the glue on the flap with the adhesive on the main body and make sure the edges are flush.

- After gluing and waiting for around 20 minutes, turn the leather piece to the front face. Take the scale and mark a sign with the needle after a 0.5 cm distance along the edge.

- Use a hammer and awl to make a punch hole at these points along the edge.

- After gluing and waiting for around 20 minutes, turn the leather piece to the front face. Take the scale and mark a sign with the needle after a 0.5 cm distance along the edge.

- Use a hammer and awl to make a punch hole at these points along the edge.

- Use the waxed thread to attach one end to the first needle and the other to the second.

- Use the double-stitch method; when you reach the point you started back, stitch three holes, snip the thread closely, and hammer down on the back stitches to set them in place, as shown in the figure.

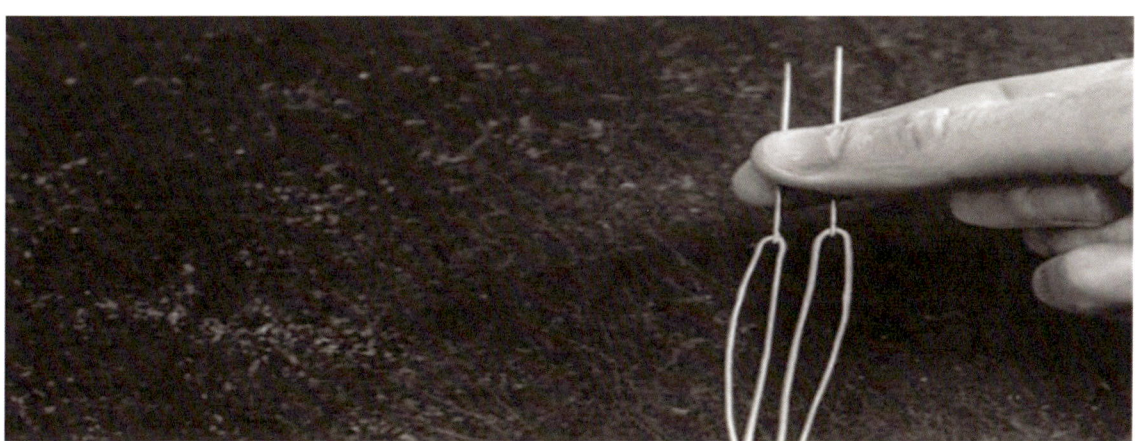

- As the last step, you can cut if any extra leather along the edge is found. Also, you can make one design and do some finishing using wax, paint, etc.

(6) Cute Heart Ring

Tools Required :

- Leather
- Ruler
- Utility Knife
- Ring template
- Scissors
- Pencil
- scotch tape
- measuring tape

Steps :

- Use the measuring tape to take measurements of the finger on which you want to wear this ring.

- Cut the design as shown where the right and left cutting when overlapped. The length should be the measurement of your finger; in this case, it is 2.5 inches.

- You can use the measuring tape to take measurements of the finger on which you want to wear this ring.

- Cut the design as shown where the right and left cutting when overlapped. The length should be the measurement of your finger; in this case, it is 2.5 inches.

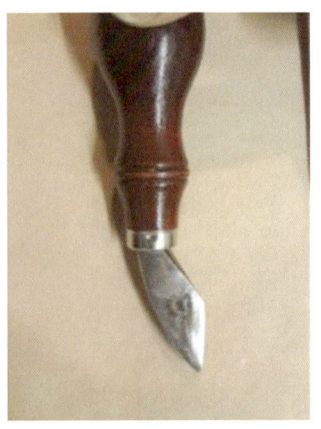

X-Acto Knife

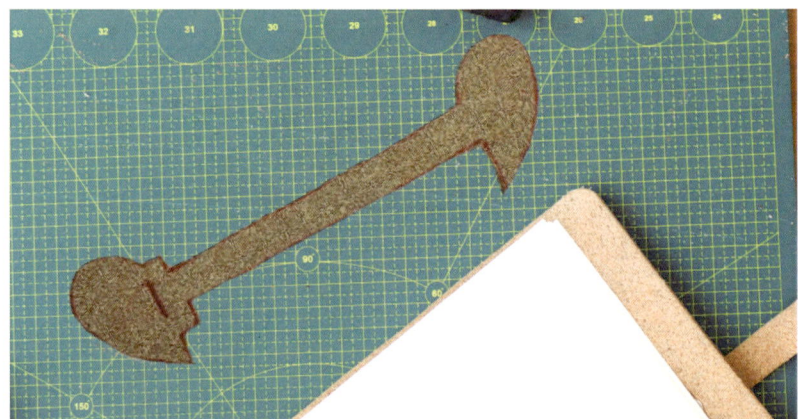

After cutting leather into shape

- Keep the template (Right & Left) on the leather piece such that the length of the strip in the middle is two and a half inches, and trace the same on the leather.

- You can use an acto knife or scissors to cut the leather in the same shape as marked in the above step.

- To make the slit fold the leather first and make it with focus using the Acto knife/scissor.

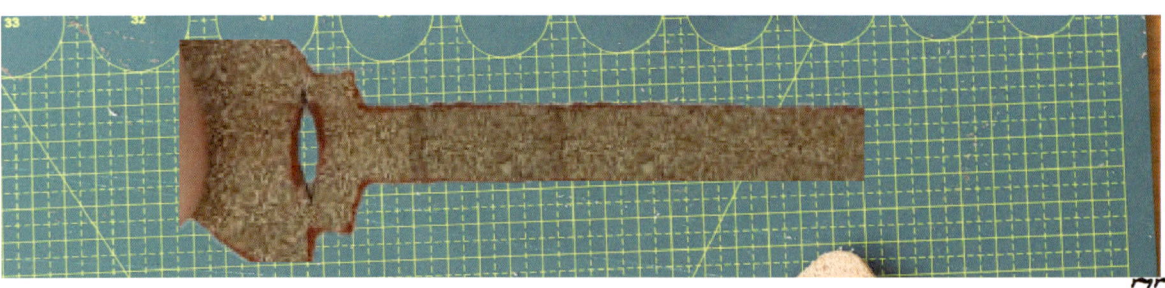

(7) Classy Coaster

Tools Required :

- Leather piece
- Glass for making a circle
- Cutting Mat
- Awl for marking circles in leather
- X- Acto blade for cutting leather
- Glue
- Mallets (hammer)
- Sewing groove for making a circle at the edge
- Manual punch for making holes
- Stitching pony for fixing leather to stitch
- Needles and threads for stitching
- Wooden Burnisher
- Leather Edge Beveler
- Burnishing Gum

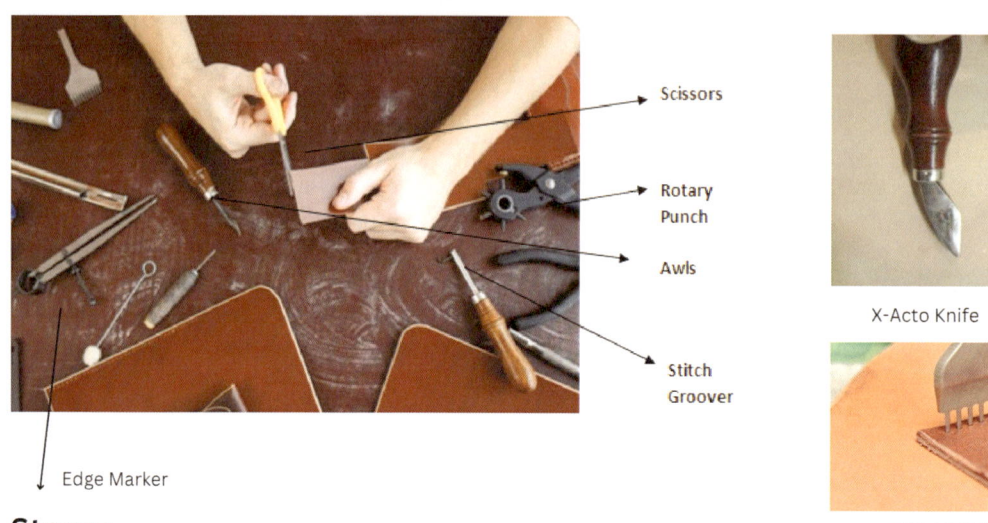

Steps :

- Take 2 rectangular pieces of leather scrap of the same dimensions.

- Next, take a glass and trace a circle in both the leather pieces using an awl.

- Take out the acto blade and cut two similar circle pieces from leather.

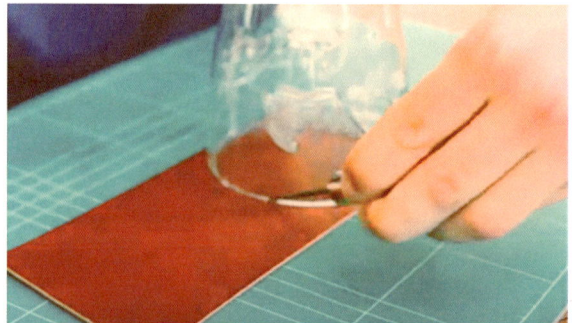 

79

- Apply glue and stick both pieces to make them thicker.

- Leave it for 20 minutes and make a circle at the edges of the glued circular piece using a sewing groover.

- Now you can use a manual punch and mallet to make holes across the circle at the edge that is in the last step.

 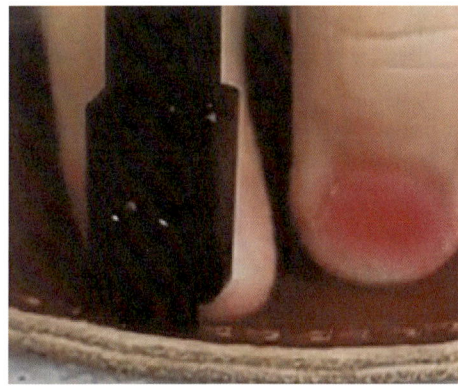

- Use two needles and waxed thread to carry the saddle stitch in the punched holes while the leather is fixed on the stitching pony.

Carry out the finishing of the edge by taking out extra leather by the edge beveler, then use a wooden beveler to smoothen the edge, and lastly apply burnishing cream.

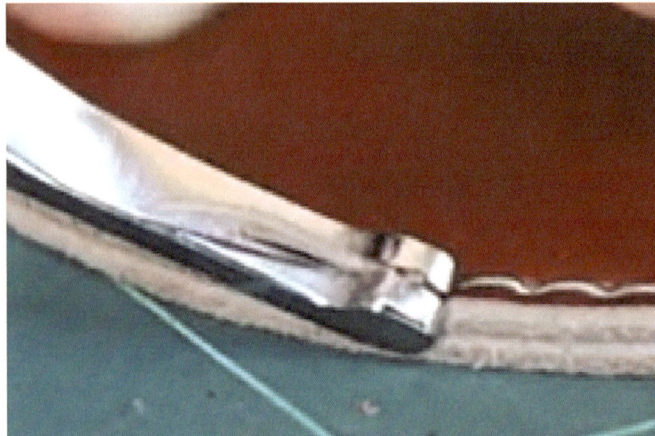

(8) Leather Desk Pad

Tools Required :

- Leather piece (four millimeters thick full grain veg tan)
- the coin for marking the curve at the edge
- Cutting Mat
- X- Acto blade/skiving knife for cutting leather
- Metal ruler
- Wooden Burnisher
- Leather Edge Beveler
- Burnishing Gum/wax/polish

Cutting Tools

Edge Beveler Tools

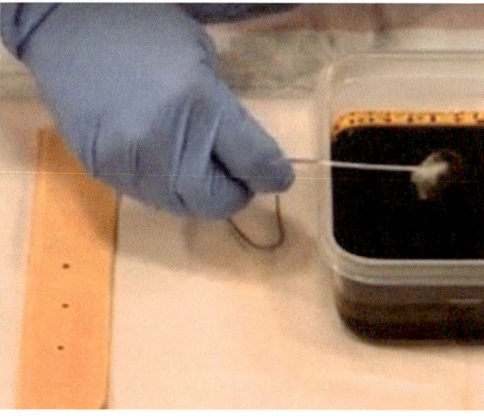

Dying using Lamb's wool

82

Steps :

- Put the leather piece on the cutting mat and take measurements of the desired length and breadth of your leather pad. In my case, it was 25x12 inches.

- Cut the leather piece using X-Acto or a skiving knife.

- Use coin and pencil to mark curved edges at all 4 corners.

- Again use an X-Acto knife or skiving knife to cut all corners into a curved shape.

- After that, use an edge beveler to cut out the extra leather along the edges.

- Apply burnishing gum/compound along the edges.

- Then, use a wooden burnisher to smoothen the edges.

- You can apply to finish wax or dye using lamb's wool if required.

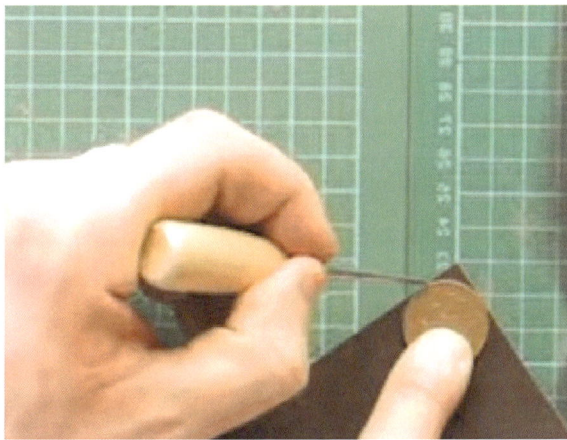
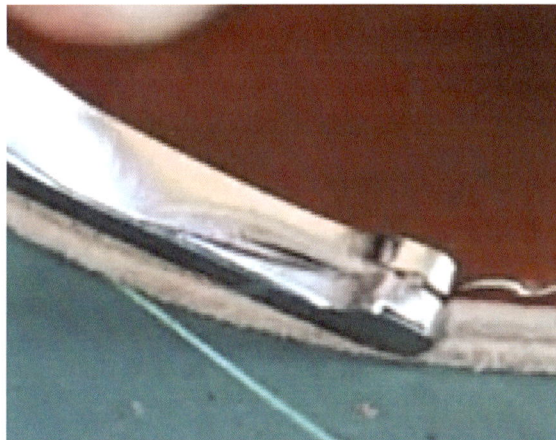

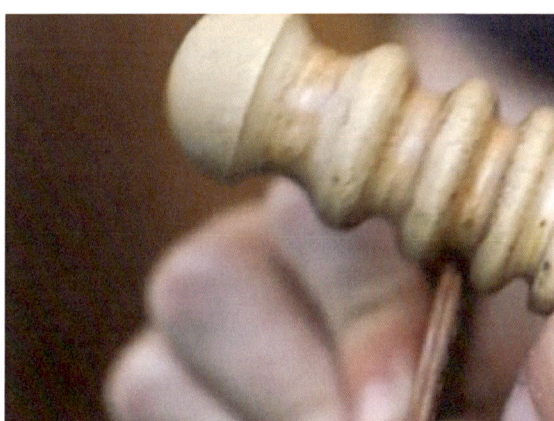

(9) Leather sunglass case

Tools Required :

- Leather piece
- A printed leather pattern on an A4 sheet
- Pencil/Pen for tracing pattern on leather
- Glue
- Cutting Mat
- Skiving Tool
- Sandpaper
- Lining Cloth
- X- Acto blade/skiving knife for cutting leather
- Metal ruler
- Manual Punch for making holes
- Wooden Burnisher
- Leather Edge Beveler
- Burnishing Gum/wax/polish
- Stitch Groover

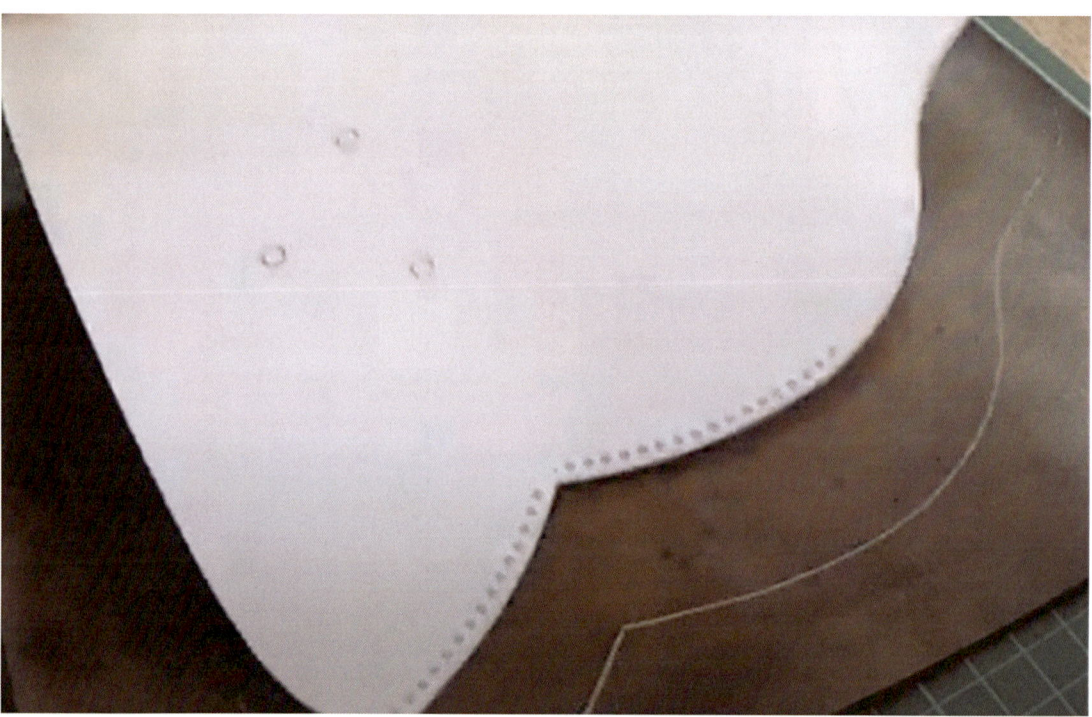

Steps :

- Take a printout of the pattern and stick it on the leather piece.
- Mark the design on the leather using a pencil/pen.
- Cut out the pattern from the leather using an X-Acto blade.

- Remove the pen/pencil mark using a wet cotton cloth.
- Apply glue to the back side of the leather and lining cloth.

- Stick the lining to the leather and cut it to match the leather's dimensions.

- Use a skiver to remove extra leather at the edge, and use sandpaper to smooth the edges.

- Use a manual punch to make holes around the edges.

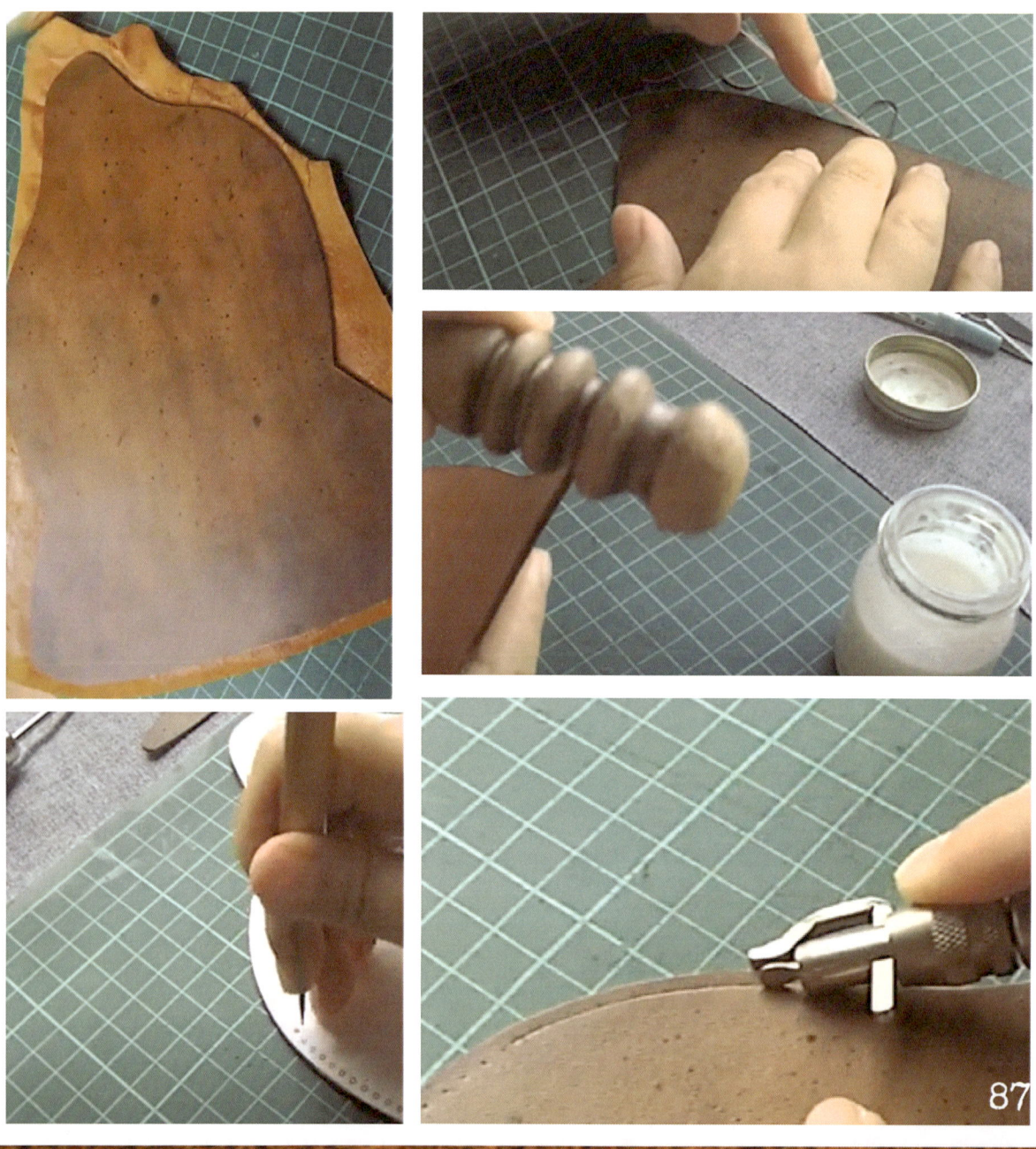

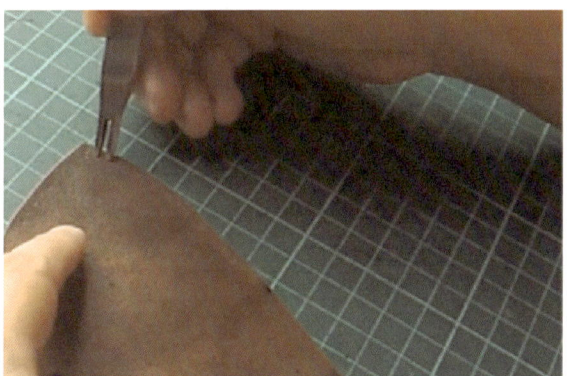

- Mark the holes as per the design and also sew holes at the border edges.

- Mark the edge border line using Stitch Groover.

- Make a hole for Sam Browne stud using a hammer and punch.

- Fold the leather and make another hole where Sam Brown Stud would be inserted.

- Carry out the saddle stitch at the edge.

{10} Card Holder

Tools Required :

- Leather
- Cutter
- Mallet/hammer
- Metal ruler
- Stitching Chisel
- Wood burnisher
- Cardboard paper (to make the pattern)
- Edge groover
- Needles and thread
- Edge Beveler
- Tokonole
- Leather glue
- Scratch awl
- Cutting board

Steps :

- Take a printout of the pattern and stick it on the leather piece.

- Mark the design on the leather using a pencil/pen.

- Cut out the pattern from the leather using an X-Acto blade. Use a metal ruler for straight cuts.

- Next, apply an edge beveler to smoothen the edges.

- Use paper clips to assemble the parts as per the design for some time to set in.

- Apply edge groover to make lines along the edge where the stitching occurs.

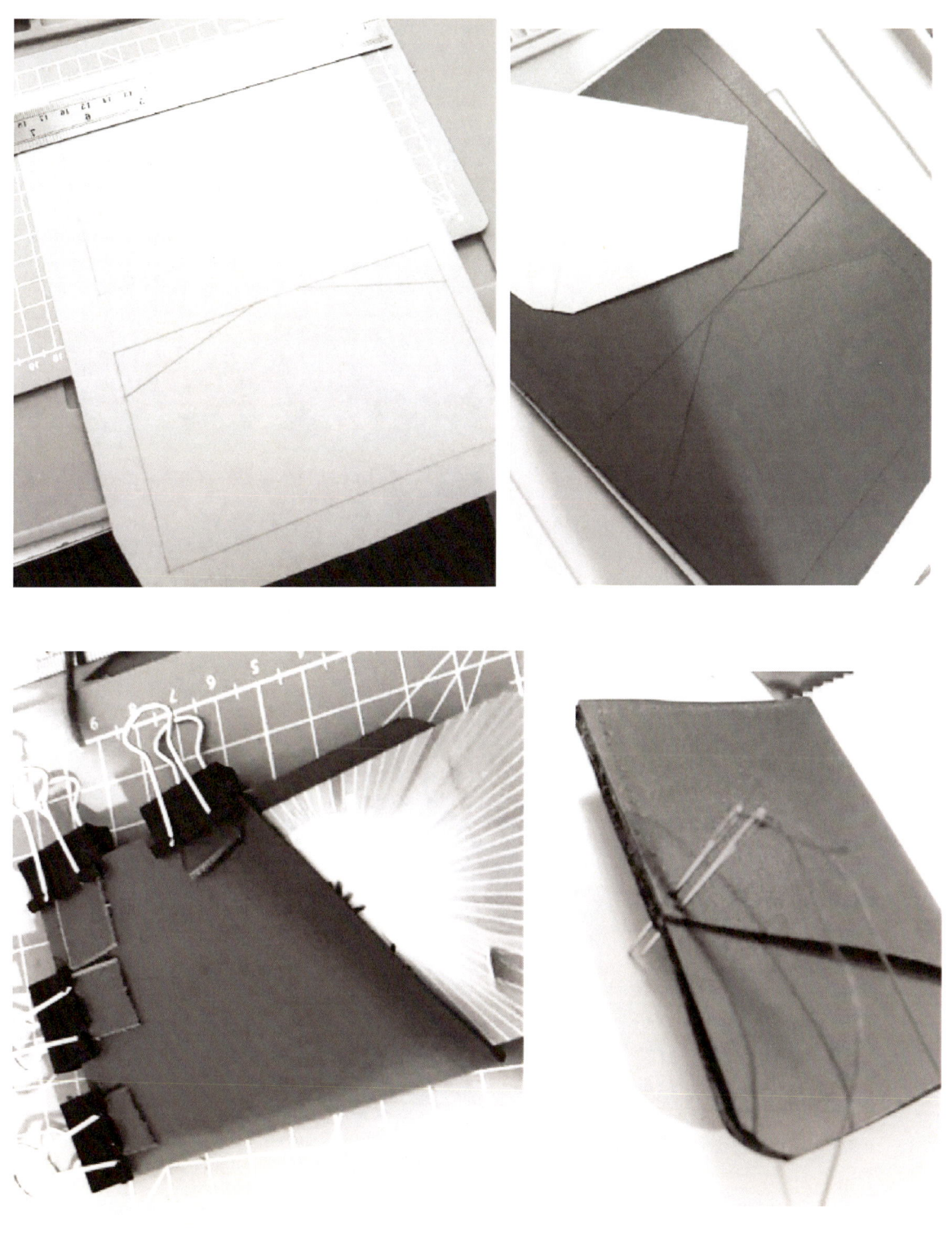

We'd Love Your Feedback!

Please let us know how we're doing by leaving us a review.

7. Tips & FAQs

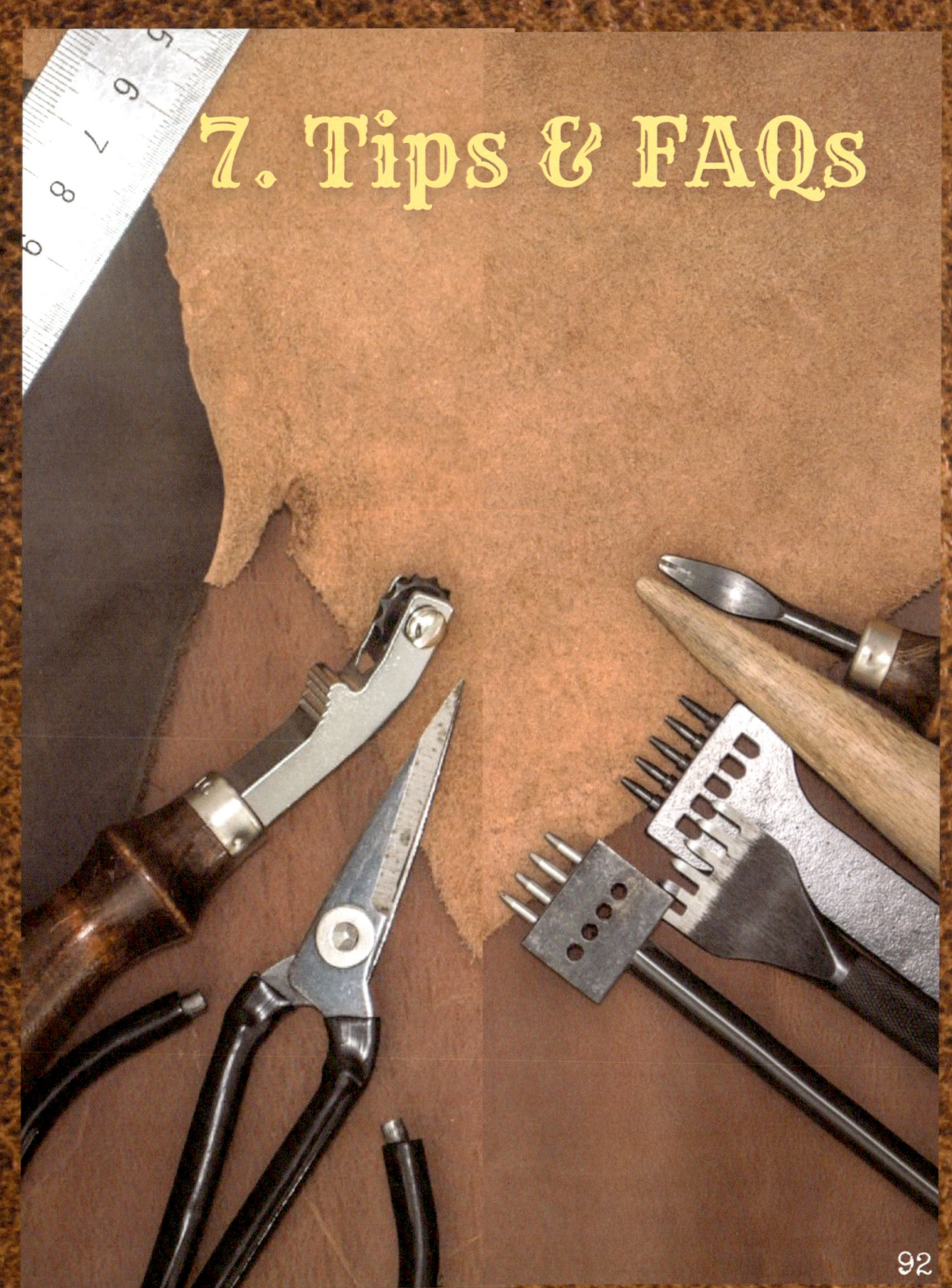

20 Tips for Beginner Leather Crafter

- **Select the ideal leather as per your project**: The kind of leather you use will impact the outcome of your project, so make sure to select the right sort of leather for your project.

- **Use sharp tools**: Dull tools can slide and cause injury, so ensure your tools are strong and in good condition.

- **Put on safety gear**: Wear gloves, eye protection, and also a mask to protect yourself from dust as well as chemicals while working with leather.

- **Cut with a steady hand**: Utilize a sharp knife and a steady hand to stay clear of injuries and clean cuts.

- **Measure twice, cut once**: Confirm your dimensions before cutting to prevent wasting leather and making errors.

- **Get a cutting board**: Utilize a cutting board or mat to protect your task surface area and extend your tools' life.

Sharpening Tool

- **Utilize the best tool for the job:** Each tool has a specific function, so ensure to use the right tool to avoid harmful products or tools.

- **Practice your stitches:** Perform your stitches on scrap leather before beginning your project to make certain tidy and stitches.

- **Use a stitching pony:** Utilize a stitching pony to hold your leather in position to prevent injuries and make the process easier.

- **Keep your workspace clean:** A tidy workspace assists you in staying organized and also protects against clutter from hindering your work.

Workdesk

- **Use a mallet** to assist in punching tools through the leather; however, use it cautiously to prevent harming the leather or tools.

- **Keep your tools organized:** Maintain them arranged and in good condition to stop crashes and lengthen their life expectancy.

- **Usage edge bevelers:** Use edge bevelers to round and smooth the sides of your leather to avoid fraying and make a professional-looking final product.

- **Prevent over-stretching leather:** Over-stretching leather can lead to it to weaken or even tear, so be gentle when working with it.

- **Usage edge slickers:** Use side slickers to polish the sides of your leather and develop a complete look.

Mallet

Edge Beveler

- **Utilize an awl:** Use an awl to make small holes in your leather for stitching or other functions.

- **Please keep your fingers clear:** Maintain your fingers free from the path of your tools to stay clear of injury.

- **Use correct lighting:** Use correct lighting to guarantee you can see what you're doing and prevent errors or injuries.

- **Utilize a leather conditioner:** Use a leather conditioner to keep your leather flexible and protect against fracturing or other damages.

- **Have a good time and be creative:** Leathercraft is a fun and creative hobby, so take pleasure in the process and don't hesitate to attempt new points and try various methods.

Beginner Frequently asked Questions (FAQs)

- **Which type of leather craft project do you want to start your journey with?**

Do you want to learn European style, Western American techniques, or rustic leatherwork?

Each approach requires different tools and methods, depending on what you're looking for in your finished product.

On the project side, do you want to build a standard leather bag or purse?

What type of stitch would you use, a basic stitch or a more complex saddle stitch, which requires much practice?

So, decide the style and expertise you want to achieve in your first learning phase. Specifically, figure out the projects you would like to work on initially. So you can focus on the exact tools and processes required in those projects.

- **Which tools you'll need for your type of leatherwork?**

Once you decide what sort of leatherwork project you intend to start your journey with, you should obtain the right tools for the work.

Start with basic tools and only purchase the ones you really need for your project. Go for better-quality tools, and always remember that only some high-quality tools are better than many low-quality ones.

In the case you choose a rustic leather project, you can make use of a lot of in-house tools. But, for more finished artwork, you would need tools like a sewing pony, swivel knife, beveler, etc.

- **Which type of leather would you need?**

Start with vegetable-tanned leather: This is the easiest to work with and is excellent for beginner projects.

Look for leather with a uniform thickness: This will make cutting and tooling the leather much easier.

Choose leather with few flaws: Seek leather that is relatively smooth and does not have too many marks, stretch marks, or other imperfections.

Decide on a color: Select a shade matching the project you want.

Choose the appropriate weight: Leather is weighed in ounces, and all projects require specific weights. For example, a little job like a purse may call for 2-3 ounces of leather, while a more extensive project like a bag might require 4-5 ounces of leather.

Purchase a little more than you require: It's always better to have a little more than to run out mid-project.

Consider the designated usage: If the job requires a great deal of punch, like a bag or belt, pick a thicker leather that will stand up well.

Think of the finish: Some leathers come naturally, while others are colored or finished with a safety coating. Think about the feel and look you desire for your task.

Examination for stretch: Pull on the leather to see how much it stretches. If it stretches excessively, it might not be suitable for your task.

Purchase from a trusted vendor: Search for a supplier specializing in leather and can advise and recommend you based on your project.

- **What should we keep in mind before stitching on initial projects?**

When it concerns stitching leather for first projects, there are a few crucial things to remember:

1. Select the ideal thread; you can choose strong and better-looking waxed polyester or all-natural linen thread, which is durable and used traditionally. Ensure your needle is sharp and strong enough to puncture with the leather.
2. Ensure your stitches are evenly spaced and tight to prevent the leather from riving.
3. Utilize a stitching pony or clamp to hold the leather in place while you function, and always verify your stitching before proceeding to the following step.

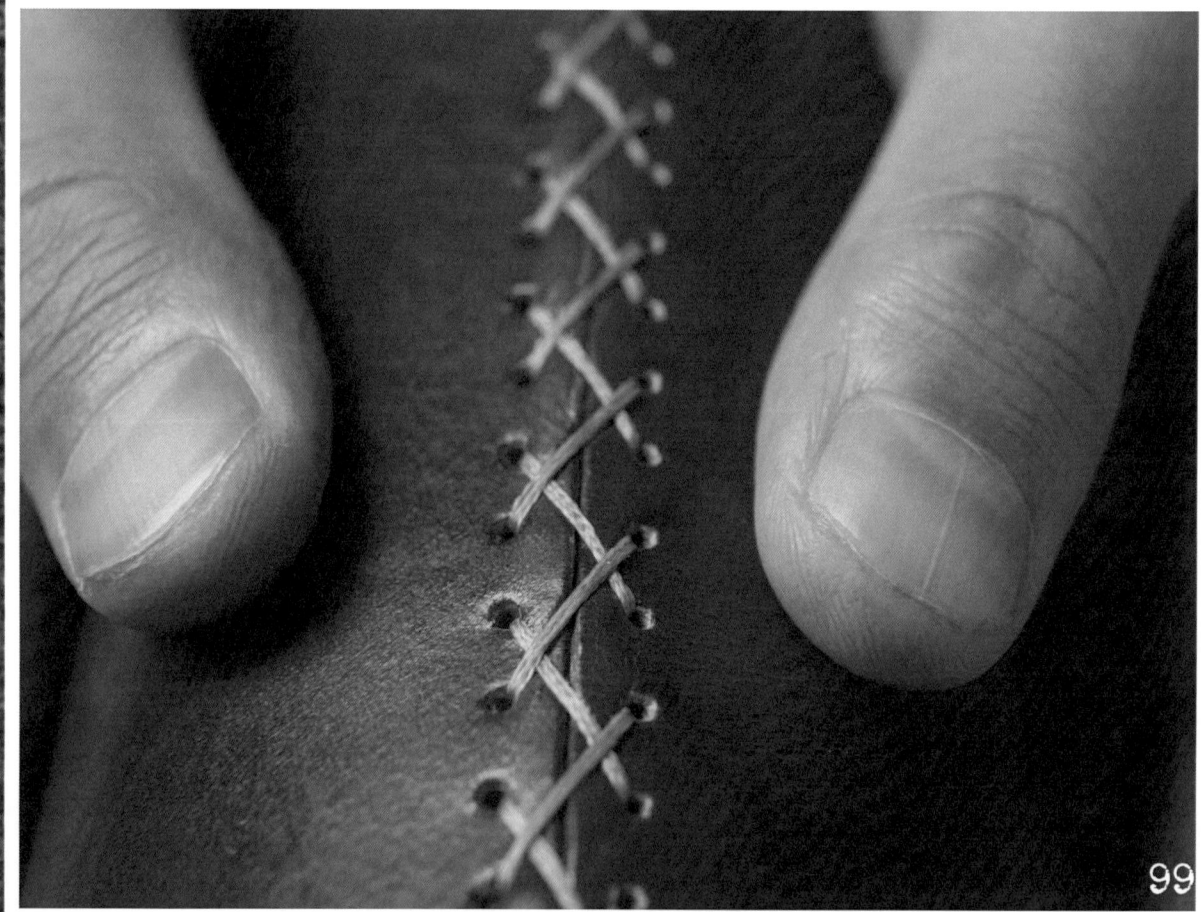

- **How do I transfer a pattern onto the leather?**

Transferring a pattern onto the leather is an essential step in leather crafting. Here are some suggestions for beginners:

- You can use tracing paper to trace the pattern onto the leather. This will allow you to transfer the pattern correctly and without smudging.

- Ensure that the leather is clean and completely dry before transferring the pattern. Any dust or wetness on the leather can influence the transfer procedure.

- If the pattern is complicated, you can utilize a tracing wheel to aid in transferring the pattern. For example, place the tracing paper on the leather and use the tracing wheel to trace the pattern lines onto the leather.

- Another approach is to utilize a transfer paper. First, put the transfer paper face down onto the leather; then, place the pattern on top of the transfer paper. Next, trace the pattern onto the transfer paper using a stylus or pen. The stress from the pen will transfer the pattern onto the leather.

- When transferring the pattern, use a leather knife or scissors to cut along the lines.

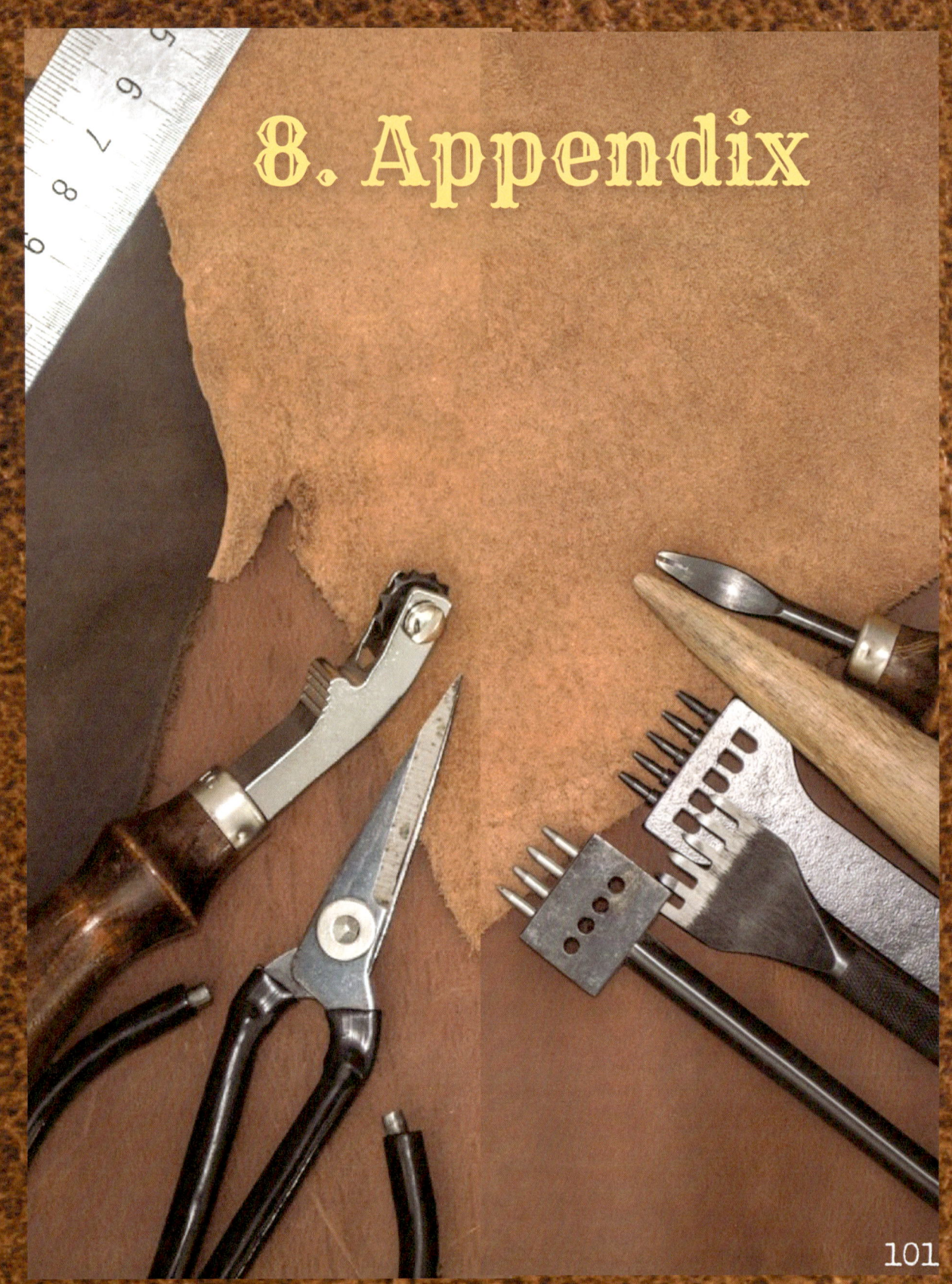

8. Appendix

APPENDIX 1 - LEATHER SUPPLIERS

Supplier Name	Website	Location
A & A CRACK & SONS LTD	www.aacrack.com	UK
A W NIDGLEY & SON LTD	www.awmidgley.co.uk	UK
ABBY ENGLAND	www.abbyengland.com	ENGLAND
ACADIA LEATHER	www.acadialeather.com	USA/ KY
AFRICAN GAME SKIN	www.africangameskin.co.UK	AFRICA
AMERICAN LEATHER DIRECT	www.aleatherd.com	USA/ KY
ARTISAN LEATHER	okwww.artisanleather.co.	UK
AVETCO LEATHER	www.avetcoinc.com	USA/ CA
BELTS PRODUCTION	www.beltsproduction.com	CROATIA
BRETTUNS VILLAGE	www.brettunsvillage.com	USA/ ME
BUCKLE GUY	www.buckleguy.com	USA/ MA
BUCKSKIN LEATHER	www.buckskinleather.com	CANADA
BUY LEATHER ONLINE	www.buyleatheronline.com	ITALY
DISTANT DRUMS	www.distantdrumsonline.com	USA / NY
DISTRIC LEATHERS	www.dublineleatherstore.com	IRELAND
DUBINE LEATHER STORE	www.fineleatherworking.com	USA/ CA

Supplier Name	Website	Location
FLETCHER	ukwww.fletcherhandmade.co.	UK
FROG JELLY LEATHER	www.frogjellyleather.com	USA/ TX
GEORDIE LEATHER	www.geordieleather.com	ENGLAND
GH LEATHERS	www.leathermerchants.com	ENGLAND
GOLIGER LEATHER	www.goligerleather.us	USA/ CA
HERMAN OAK LEATHER	http://www.hermannoakleather.com	USA/ MO
HIDE HOUSE	www.hidehouse.com	USA/ CA
IDENTITY LEATHERCRAFT	www.identityleathercraft.com	UK
ITAL LEATHER EXPERIENCE	www.italleatherexperience.com	ITALY
J. WOOD LEATHER LTD	www.jwoodleathers.co.uk	UK
LAEDERIET	www.laederiet.dk	DENMARK
LE PREVO	www.leprevo.co.uk	UK
LEATHER4CRAFT	www.leathercraft.co.uk	UK
LEATHER COSMOS	www.leathercosmos.com	GREECE
LEATHER CRAFT PATTERN	www.leathercraftpattern.com	HONG KONG
LEATHER DIRECT	www.leatherdirect.com.au	AUSTRAILIA

103

APPENDIX 2 - INCHES TO MILLIMETER TABLE

Inches	MM	Inches	MM
1/4"	6	5"	127
1/2"	13	5 1/4"	133
3/4"	19	5 1/2"	140
1"	25	5 3/4"	146
1 1/4"	32	6"	152
1 1/2"	38	6 1/4"	159
1 3/4"	44	6 1/2"	165
2"	51	6 3/4"	171
2 1/4"	57	7"	178
2 1/2"	64	7 1/4"	184
2 3/4"	70	7 1/2"	191
3"	76	7 3/4"	197
3 1/4"	83	8"	203
3 1/2"	89	8 1/4"	210
3 3/4"	95	8 1/2"	216
4"	102	8 3/4"	222
4 1/4"	108	9"	229
4 1/2"	114	9 1/4"	235
4 3/4"	121	9 1/2"	241
5"	127	9 3/4"	248
5 1/4"	133	10"	254

Appendix 3 - Online Resources

Leather Craft Magazines

1. Shop Talk: https://shoptalk-magazine.com/

2. Leather Crafters Journal: https://leathercraftersjournal.com/

3. Euro Leather Norway: http://euroleather.no/

4. Russian Leather Crafting Magazine: http://www.en.leathercrafting-journal.ru/

5. Waxing the Thread U.K: https://gdhleathercourses.co.uk/

Free Downloadable Patterns

You can find free patterns for non-commercial and personal use on the sites below. Read the copyright document for each one carefully.

1. Leathercraft Pattern.com
2. Leathercove.com
3. Worldofpatterns.com
4. jlsleather.com

APPENDIX 4 - GLOSSARY

Grain: The leather's top layer has the most sturdiness and strength.

Flesh side: The underside of the leather.

Dye: A fluid made use of to color the leather.

Edge beveler: A tool used to bevel the edges of the leather to make them smoother.

Burnishing: A process of smoothing and polishing the edges of the leather after they have been beveled.

Stitching chisel: A tool used to create holes in the leather for stitching.

Awl: A pointed tool used to pierce leather holes for stitching or other objectives.

Skiving: A procedure of thinning down the leather for a smoother finish.

Veg-tanned leather: Leather that has been tanned using vegetable-based materials.

Split leather: Leather split from the top layer to develop a thinner and much less durable product.

Saddle stitch: A solid, two-needle sewing method used to sew leather with each other.

Leather conditioner: A product utilized to moisturize and shield the leather from drying.

Mallet: A hammer-like tool used to strike leather crafting tools and punches.

Strap cutter: A tool used to cut leather straps or strips of consistent size.

Rivet: A bolt used to hold two items of leather with each other without stitching.

Leather Skiving - A technique to slim the leather from the edges for smoother edges and a better appearance.

Edge Beveling - A strategy to round off the edges of the leather to get rid of intensity and also avoid it from fraying.

Leather Dyeing - The procedure of coloring the leather, using dyes to attain the desired color or color.

Leather Staining - A strategy used to develop a one-of-a-kind and rustic look on the leather by applying numerous stains and colors in a specific manner.

Leather Tooling - A procedure of developing layouts or patterns on the leather surface using stamping tools, swivel knives, and mallets.

Leather Splitting - A technique used to split a piece of leather into thinner areas to achieve the wanted thickness for a particular project.

Leather Punching - Making holes in the leather using punch tools for stitching, lacing, or adding hardware like snaps and rivets.

Leather Skiving Knife - A specialized knife for thinning the leather from the edges.

Leather Awl - A tool for making small holes and noting lines on the leather.

www.ingramcontent.com/pod-product-compliance
Lightning Source LLC
Chambersburg PA
CBRC090836010526
44107CB00051B/1635